# Fire
# on the Hills

# Fire
# on the Hills

**The Rochunga Pudaite Story**

**Joe Musser
and
James & Marti Hefley**

**Tyndale House Publishers, Inc.
Wheaton, Illinois**

**Library of Congress Cataloging-in-Publication Data**

Musser, Joe.
    Fire on the hills: the Rochunga Pudaite Story
    by Joe Musser and James & Marti Hefley.
       p.  cm.
    ISBN 0-8423-1891-7 (softcover : alk. paper)
    1. Pudaite, Rochunga.  2. Missionaries--India, Northeastern--
Biography.  3. Bibles for the World (Organization)--History.
I. Hefley, James C. II. Hefley, Marti. III. Title.
BV3269.P8M87  1998
266´.0092--dc21
[B]                98-37368

Printed in the United States of America

06 05 04 03 02 01 00 99 98
 8  7  6  5  4  3  2  1

# Contents

# Acknowledgments

In compiling this authorized biography, there are a number of people who deserve our specific recognition and sincere gratitude.

Joe Musser is an author and media consultant, a close friend who has known us for thirty years. He and his wife, Nancy, are longtime board members of Bibles For The World. No one knows our experiences and sufferings or our failures and successes as well as Joe does.

Jim and Marti Hefley, who wrote an earlier biography, *God's Tribesman*, provided a wealth of research and material for this book, which is an extension of their effort by bringing our story up to date.

Of course, there would be no story in the first place without Watkin R. Roberts, the missionary who first came to our tribe in 1910. The Hmars are deeply indebted for his love and sacrifice in bringing the gospel to northeast India.

Dr. Carl Wenger, a retired surgeon from Little Rock, Arkansas, and his dear wife, Lib, are our close friends and confidants. Dr. Wenger is chairman emeritus of Bibles For The World's board of directors. His godly counsel and wise leadership were invaluable to us during his tenure as board chairman of our organization.

Dr. Paul Roberts, a retired missionary physician and the son of Watkin R. Roberts, has been a wonderful friend and serves as a member of the board of directors for Bibles For The World (Canada).

There are others, too, without whose help there would be no book, whose influence upon our lives and experience has been significant and life changing:

Dr. V. Raymond Edman, late president and chancellor, Wheaton College;

Mrs. Indira Gandhi, former prime minister of India;

Billy Graham, international evangelist;

Evert and Lorraine Peterson, Wilmar, Minnesota;

Doug and Faith Mains, Wheaton, Illinois;

Rev. Ruoleneikhum Pakhuongte, president, Evangelical Free Church of India;

Dr. Bob Pierce, founder of World Vision;

V. V. Purie, chairman, Thompson Press and a founder of *India Today;*

Ray and Edie Quiggin, board members emeritus, BFW;

Bernie and Lee Reese, board members emeritus, BFW;

Rev. Lalthankhum Sinate, vice president, Partnership Mission Society;

Dr. Ken Taylor, author of *The Living Bible*, founder of Tyndale House Publishers

There are countless other friends and supporters whose memory, friendship and partnership we treasure, but it would be impossible to include them all.

For whatever encouragement, inspiration or challenge that readers may find within the pages of this book, we offer God the glory.

Rochunga and Mawii Pudaite

# Introduction

Rochunga Pudaite, the subject of this inspiring story, has been a neighbor of mine for many years, living two houses away along with his wife, Mawii, and their fine children.

I remember so well the day Ro came to tell me about the idea God had given him of reaching India through mailboxes. He pointed out that millions of names and addresses were readily available from the Indian telephone directories.

Although it was more expensive to mail New Testaments from the U.S. than to mail them from inside India, there would be extra interest for recipients when an unexpected package arrived from America. And so the experiment was tried, resulting in thousands of responses from people asking for more information about our Lord Jesus Christ.

Now this creative idea of using telephone books for names and addresses has gone forward in over one hundred other countries and scores of languages in an ongoing effort to let the whole world know about Jesus.

I have a special interest in Ro and Mawii because of their recurrent use of easy-to-read New Testaments, often *The Living Bible*. They want those who know little about our Lord to be able to easily read a Bible they can clearly understand.

Their life ministry has been similar to mine—to tell people everywhere about the Savior.

Kenneth N. Taylor

# Chapter One
## *Fire on the Hills*

As Chawnga's family took up their packs to leave their village of Senvon in Manipur, northeast India, little five-year-old Rochunga saw a church elder pulling at his father's arm. "Please, Chawnga. You must leave your family here or else your wife will die on this hard journey."

"We must go," Rochunga's father replied simply. "God will help her."

But jeering laughter rolled through the rest of the crowd as the family members took up their packs. One person said, "This man is crazy!" Others murmured similar derisive comments. Little "Ro" indignantly kicked at dirt outside the familiar bamboo hut that was no longer his home.

"Why do they say such mean things about Father?" Ro asked his older brother, Ramlien. But Ramlien appeared just as puzzled and confused as Ro was.

It had seemed clear to young Ro when his father explained to the family how he felt God calling him to move from Senvon to Phulpui, a long three-day journey on foot through the mountain ranges. In Phulpui there was no church and Chawnga was going there to minister to those people.

The church elder tried once more to coax his friend. "Chawnga, you must not take your wife, Daii, and the children. Leave them here. Your wife will surely die if you go."

1

Then little Ro saw the determined look in his father's dark eyes.

"We *must* go. God will care for Daii."

Ro's ailing mother rose slightly from the litter upon which she rested. "Yes," she whispered weakly, "God will help me."

The boy watched his father gently take his mother's hand and lift her to a standing position. The crowd murmured softly in quiet amazement. This act itself made a statement.

"Make way, my friends," Chawnga said quite decisively. "The sun grows warm, and we must go."

The crowd parted, making an opening for Chawnga and his family. As his father led them, Ro took his mother's hand as if to lend her his own strength. She had been ill for as long as he could remember.

The villagers began to call after them, *"Damtakin!"* (the Hmar equivalent of "farewell").

*"Damtakin!"* Chawnga called out. The word echoed from everyone now, and even little Ro shouted *damtakin* as he turned and waved. They were on their way.

Ro still smarted from the ridicule of those who called his father crazy, and he pulled himself up tall, straightened his shoulders, and briskly pumped his short legs up and down in order to keep up. Somehow his mother had found strength to match the stride of her husband.

After just a few minutes of walking, Ro felt his mother's hand become hot and damp. Peering up at her anxiously, he saw that her face glistened with perspiration. Then when he heard her labored breathing he wondered, *How much farther can she go?*

They had walked nearly a half mile out of the village when suddenly his mother stopped, swayed, and collapsed on the ground.

"Mother!" Ro cried, "Are you all right?"

Ro moved back as his father took command. Chawnga took a gourd jug and poured water over his wife's head. Then, his heart pounding, Ro heard his father pray. Raising his arms and looking to heaven, Chawnga implored, "Great God, you have called me to far regions. Yet you have also given me a family, and I cannot abandon them. Give Daii strength to go with me. Lord, let her *walk!*"

Young Rochunga watched as his mother's eyelids fluttered lightly. She looked up at her husband, and they exchanged loving smiles. Weakly, she told him, "Let us walk on."

Amazingly, Daii found the strength to stand and walk again. Ro again clung to her hand. This time, Chawnga put his arm around his wife, and using his right hand for his walking staff, they set out again.

At the brow of a hill, they paused to let a breeze cool them. They looked across the wide expanse of mountains and jungle forests that comprised their land of northeast India. In that spring of 1932, it was an untamed part of India, populated by chattering monkeys, huge roving herds of wild elephants, fierce Bengal tigers, giant pythons, and strange tribes hardly known to the outside world.

It was not too many years ago, when his father was Ro's age, that his people (the Hmar tribe) had been considered savage headhunters. The British colonial rulers had tried to keep people out of the Hmar tribal lands. Now, as his father had told him many times, most of the Hmar people were no longer terribly fierce savages. They had turned from headhunting to hearthunting when they became believers in Jesus Christ, following the Christian God.

The family walked an amazing ten miles that day, through clouds of mosquitoes and ambushes of painful bloodsucking leeches. They stopped only for brief rest periods, and when they finally stopped for the night in the village of Lungthulien, they were all exhausted. Ro immediately fell asleep after a light supper.

The next morning he awoke with a start, not knowing at first where he was. It was a strange hut, but then he remembered their journey the day before. Looking around, Ro spied Daii's bed. He got up and went cautiously over to where she lay.

"Mother," Ro said, "are you still alive?"

"Yes, my son," she said smiling. "I am still living." To prove it she squeezed his hand. Then, to everyone's amazement, she not only got up from her sickbed, but she began to prepare breakfast! The villagers were shocked as they watched Daii get the water and boil it for tea and rice, then cook the food herself.

After breakfast they resumed their hard journey. Along the trail, Ro slipped, sprained his ankle, and had to be carried to the swift-running Barak River. There, he sat quietly on a bamboo raft as they were poled across the stream.

In just three days the family reached Phulpui, where a curious crowd met them, then followed them to the small hut that Chawnga had built on a previous trip. Chawnga explained to the villagers that he had come from Senvon to build a church. The people listened to the preacher and watched as Chawnga's family inspected their new home. It stood on stilts and had a split bamboo floor, walls, and a thatched roof.

The *songka*, open porch, was used for drying clothes, relaxing, or entertaining friends in the evening. Behind the *songka* was a *sumphuk*, an enclosed veranda where women pounded rice and men did small carpentry tasks and other work.

In the main room was a *tap*, a large raised hearth made of hard, kneaded clay that was compacted into a wooden frame. In the center of the *tap* was a *lungdhu*, the name for three fixed stones upon which the cooking pots sat. A few feet beyond the *tap* was an area for sleeping.

The porters arrived with the family's goods and were surprised not only that Daii was still alive, but seemed unusually well. In fact, Ro watched proudly as she served them tea when they finished the delivery.

Later he sat quite still as both his parents offered prayers of thanksgiving for Daii's healing.

The climate of Phulpui was not nearly as nice as in Senvon. In this lower altitude, the sun was hotter and the clouds of angry mosquitoes were much thicker at night. But such minor discomforts did not stop Ro's father from building a bamboo church on a plot of land that the local chief had given him at the edge of the village.

The little ten-by-fifteen-foot building was finished in time for Sunday services. Ro and Ramlien washed their faces, carefully slicked down their hair with a comb and pulled on shorts and shirts. Before leaving home, Ro peered down into the big black *sumbel* (water pot) on the front

5

porch. The water reflected his smiling face. He did look grand!

But as they marched proudly along the dusty road toward the bamboo church, he heard the laughs and giggles from the village boys. One shrill voice yelled, "Look at them! They let the cows lick their heads!"

Ro was so chagrined that he quickly mussed his hair and rushed into the church. "What happened to your hair?" his father demanded. When Ro explained, his father simply said, "Go and comb it again. It will look fine."

When the service began, only Chawnga's family and two other people were there. But the preacher was not deterred and he thundered his message as if a thousand people were present. With only bamboo walls to keep in the sound, most of the villagers also heard Chawnga's Sunday sermon.

Ro grinned; the people didn't know what a powerful voice his father had! The preacher told them how the love of God had turned his tribe from headhunting to Christianity.

"Over a hundred years ago," he told them, "a Hmar wise man foretold the coming of white-skinned people with guns. They came and conquered our land. This same wise man said that other white people would follow the ones with guns, and these people would tell us of a new religion, one not requiring the sacrifice of animals or chickens.

"This new religion was brought first to Senvon, from where my father and I came. We have now come to tell you about the path that takes you to meet the true God. Follow this trail, and you will know forgiveness for your evil deeds and find happiness for living. Listen to what God's Word says. . . ."

By delivering such powerful sermons and by visiting every home in the village, Chawnga had a sizable congregation by the time they celebrated Christmas, the birthday of the Savior to the world.

\* \* \*

By the end of the second year, the small church had been enlarged twice. Chawnga began to visit other villages and soon was an itinerant preacher for some twenty other villages in the Vangai range. Sometimes Daii accompanied him, while her mother-in-law cared for their young children.

Frequently Ro's parents would bring home orphans after their evangelistic trips to other villages. These orphans were accepted as if they were members of the family, receiving food and shelter from them along with genuine loving care.

Chawnga was often gone for long periods of time, but when he was home, he always had time for his children. He taught his sons how to make traps to catch game, to fish, and to hunt. He also taught them the ancient skills passed down by his father and ancestors—storytelling, singing, and dances. And before bedtime Ro often heard his father tell them a story. Most of the time, the stories had a moral, though Ro was captivated by the drama as much as by the point.

So it was natural for Ro to ask one evening, "My father, who first told you of the gospel?"

Chawnga smiled, for he never tired of telling that story. "Well, my son," he began, "when I was young, a friend and I walked six days to the village of Aijal. We hoped to sell chickens and make a profit. Along a path we met three strange, white-skinned men with light hair and eyes.

"This was my first encounter with white foreign missionaries. Later, I was told by the Lushai that the oldest of them was called 'Mr. Old White Man,' the second was named 'Mr. Other White Man,' and the third one, 'Mr. Young White Man.'"

Chawnga referred to the tribal tradition of using descriptions as names. He continued his story: "They promised to buy our chickens for a fair price if we would follow them to their mission home. We did, and they kept their word about buying our chickens.

"Then, sometime later I met another Mr. Young Man, who came to Senvon and told us that he had come to India from a far-off land called Wales, in the Year of the Flowering Bamboo (1908). He said his White Man name was Watkin Roberts, but we called him *Pu Tlangval* (Mr. Young Man).

"Mr. Young Man was kind to us. He did not seem as foreign as the others, for his hair was black like ours. And he came and lived among us in bamboo huts, not like the white foreigners who lived in mission compounds.

"It was Mr. Young Man who told us about Jesus. In those days foreigners were afraid of our people—they feared that we would chop off their heads! But that did not stop Mr. Young Man. He traveled everywhere to tell our people about Jesus and the one true God.

"Once when he heard that a dying Lushai chief was having his slaves buried alive with him, which was the custom, Mr. Young Man traveled day and night to get there before it could happen. When he arrived, the slaves were already in the grave, buried to their waists. He stopped the burial and had his own native helpers dig them out. And no one laid a hand on him."

Sitting beside his father, Ro sighed in admiration. "Mr. Young Man must have been very brave, Father."

"He was, my son. He defied the British agent when he sneaked into Hmar territory to tell us about God. He sent copies of John's Gospel written in the Lushai language to us. One day he was invited by our chief, Kamkholun, to come to Senvon and tell the meaning of the book to us.

"But the British agent warned him that he would be killed. He reminded Mr. Young Man that foreigners were not allowed in the headhunting territories. But instead of killing him, the people of Senvon gave him gifts and listened respectfully to his message.

"He told us that Jesus was born as a baby in a tiny village like ours and grew up to be a man. Then Jesus was put to death as a sacrifice for our sins.

"He talked to us a very long time about believing in Jesus, God's Son, and about taking God's ways as our own. I liked what he said, for I knew the ways of our tribe were bad, and when I thought of our taking the heads of our enemies, I knew it was wrong. Even your own grandfather took human heads and hung them proudly upon his house.

"But I did not accept Christianity just then. I felt my friends would laugh at me if I did not follow our traditions. And the tribal elders would rebuke me if I did not offer sacrifices. If I followed

Jesus, then the tribal priest would not help me when I got sick. My friends would not invite me to their parties. Mr. Young Man even told us that a follower of Jesus should not drink rice beer.

"I told Mr. Young Man that I could not be a follower of Jesus, but I kept thinking about what he had said. And I listened some more," Chawnga said quietly. "Not too long after that, I became a Christian.

"Mr. Young Man could only stay in Senvon for five days but promised to return if possible. But the British agent never let him come back to us. We who had become Christians had to travel to him for further training."

Chawnga stood up and stretched. "But that is another story," he said, smiling. "It is time for children to be in bed."

Ro lay on his mat and tried to think what it must have been like to *not* know of Jesus. All his young life he had heard Bible stories. His mother had sung hymns and Christian songs to him since he was a baby. Even his name, Rochunga, (meaning "inheritor of highest treasure") had a Christian significance. His mother had told him many times how he'd gotten his name: "Your grandfather, my father," she had said, "became a Christian about the time you were born. He wanted you to be named as a testimony of what he had received from God."

Then, still recalling the story of how Christianity had ignited his tribe and spread as a fire on the hills to an entire people group, Ro drifted off to sleep.

\*        \*        \*

When his father was away traveling, Ro and his brother were responsible for milking the family cows each morning and evening. In the hot, humid climate the animals gave little milk, but so long as they were not visited by bears or tigers, milking was an uneventful chore.

Ro liked fishing and catching wild fowl more than his milking chores. His real forte was setting snares for the white jungle rats that were considered such a Hmar delicacy.

Several years went by like this, and as he grew older, Ro's rat catching drew an invitation to join the village gang. Anxious to prove he was no sissy, Ro helped the gang set snares for the women carrying firewood from the jungle or water from the nearby stream. Although Ro's conscience bothered him, he pretended to enjoy watching a helpless woman squirming to free her feet from the snare.

The gang leader, Hmingte, demanded absolute loyalty from his followers. One test was for the boys to skin live rats with their teeth while the rodents squealed in agony. Ro knew his parents would never approve of such awful and bizarre acts. Nor did he want to deceive his parents, for until he joined the gang he'd always been a respectful and obedient son. Yet, he seemed to be trapped by the peer pressure of the gang from which it was becoming more and more difficult to escape.

The breaking point came one day in the jungle. Hmingte ordered the boys to climb a tall tree as a test of their loyalty and courage. But as soon as they were up to its highest point, Hmingte began chopping it down. When the boys cried for him to stop, he threatened to chop off the feet of any boy who tried to come down.

So the terrified boys clung desperately to the slender tree trunk as it shuddered with each blow of the axe. As the final blow landed, the wood splintered loudly, and the tree began to lean. First it started slowly, then as gravity took over, it fell quickly and mightily with the screaming boys clinging to it.

Ro hit the ground with a thud. He was somewhat cushioned by branches when he fell but was momentarily stunned, with the wind knocked out of him. Finally, he got up, badly bruised but with nothing broken. He looked around for his friends. The others were likewise stunned and bruised but picked themselves up. All except one.

"Trana!" Ro called out. His friend was lying on the ground motionless. "Trana!" he cried again. Even Hmingte became frightened now, for Trana was absolutely still. They all feared he was dead.

"Don't any of you tell what happened!" Hmingte warned them. "If any of you dare to tell, I will kill you!" With that he ran off into the jungle.

After several agonizing moments Trana moaned faintly and moved his head. After a few more minutes he was able to sit up. The boys discovered that he had also survived with no broken bones. However, Ro was so thoroughly frightened by the experience that he decided to quit the gang.

A few days later Ro's father returned from a trip and took his son fishing. They walked to the river and drained a small pool so they could wade through the water and chase the fish into the pool, where they could catch them by hand.

As Ro felt among the rocks for the fish, he asked Chawnga, "My father, why must you be gone so often?"

"My son, you know there are many of our people who have not heard that God sent his Son to die so they might have everlasting life. I must go and tell them."

Ro grabbed a shiny *ngahra* and tossed it flopping onto the riverbank. *I've known that all my life,* he thought solemnly, *but it has made no difference in my life. I am no better than the other boys in the gang who have not heard about Jesus.*

Chawnga seemed to sense that something was troubling his son. "Let us rest," he said. "The fish will not go anywhere."

The two of them sat on the grassy riverbank. Ro watched a noisy and mischievous monkey swing in the trees above them. He waited for his father to say something, but Chawnga was silent. Finally he went back to catching fish, and soon they had enough for their evening meal.

Although Ro had not confided his inner feelings to his father, he was glad for having been with him.

The next Sunday evening, after ending his sermon, Chawnga gave an evangelistic invitation. "If any of you truly believe and want to follow Jesus, you should not be ashamed to say so publicly," he told them.

Ro felt his face flush and his stomach begin to churn. It was as if God himself, through Chawnga, was talking to him alone. Ro listened and was overwhelmed by guilt and remorse. He slowly stepped to the front of the small church. "My father," the boy said softly. Then he added solemnly, "I believe, and I have given my name to

Jesus." (The tribespeople felt that when they gave their names to another, they were trusting the recipient to prove worthy of their confidence. That was why they were always reluctant to use their names in conversation, preferring that friends do it for them indirectly.)

"Have you truly given your name to Jesus?" Chawnga asked the boy.

Ro nodded. "If it is written in the Book, as you say, that he will forgive all those who ask him, then he has taken away each and every sin. God would not lie."

"Yes," Chawnga said, smiling. "It is written in his Book."

\*       \*       \*

Some days later Chawnga began to talk of a great need in the Hmar tribe. His words were directed to ten-year-old Rochunga. "My son, you know that we do not have God's Word in our own language. We have only the Lushai New Testament, and sadly many Hmars do not understand it. Someone must write God's Word in Hmar."

"Can you do it, my father?" Ro asked.

Chawnga shook his head sadly. "I do not have the learning. Nor does any other Hmar. And the missionaries with learning are not allowed to live among us." A long pause stretched between father and son.

"How much learning is required?" Ro finally asked.

"More than you can receive in our little village school. To get such learning would require going far away. You can be the one, Rochunga." He let the meaning of his words sink in, then added, "Your mother and I have prayed and dedicated you to God for this great work, but we will not send you away against your will. You must *want* to do this, to get an education for the making of a Hmar Bible."

Ro sat very still. He had heard Hmars speak with awe of the knowledge of an educated man. His uncle had told him that if someone were to finish primary school, high school, college, and then earn what he called a master's degree, that person would know *everything*. "Why, he could stand on the root of any tree and know how many leaves were hanging on its branches!" his uncle had reported.

Ro looked up at his father and said with unusual solemnity, "I think I would like to be an educated man."

So it was that Chawnga and Daii arranged for Ro to attend the mission school, some ninety-six miles away, in Churachandpur in the east, toward Burma. It was a great sacrifice for the family. Even with Ro working to pay his own room and board, Chawnga would have to contribute one-fourth of his monthly salary as tuition.

Ro was excited about going to school until he learned how far he would have to walk through the jungle. "Look how short and puny my legs are," he said. "A journey of ninety-six miles will take many, many days!"

Chawnga ran his hand up the short, brown legs and raised his eyebrows. "My, what muscles you have! I never noticed how strong your legs are." Ro thought that maybe he had misjudged his legs after his father's look at them. Maybe he was stronger and more capable than he thought.

His confidence dwindled a few days later when it came time for him to leave. It wasn't just the long walk. He would have to be away from home for ten long months at a time. Already he was homesick.

And then there was the real possibility of meeting a fierce Bengal tiger on the trail. His father promised to walk with him on the first trip to show him the way, but even Chawnga was no match for a tiger. When Ro confided his fear, Chawnga assured him that God would protect them. But Ro wasn't so certain.

As if to confirm his worst fears, a few days later he and Trana were driving the cattle home when they saw a reddish flash in the high grass. Then a cow bellowed loudly in great fear. Suddenly, within seconds, the cattle stampeded. *A tiger!* Ro stood motionless for a moment, eyeing the great brute standing on the far side of the road in a hunting stance, crouched with tail low as if to jump at him.

Ro tried to shout, but fear paralyzed his throat. Then a verse his father had taught him came instantly to mind: *"Though I walk through the valley of the shadow of death, I will fear no evil."*

Suddenly he heard a man call, "Clap your hands and shout!" He and Trana did as he ordered, and the tiger loped away, but his fearful presence was still in the air.

Sometime later, Ro was still thinking about the ninety-six-mile trip to Churachandpur for schooling. Pondering these concerns one Sunday evening in church, Ro listened as his father translated a verse from the Lushai Bible: "Having loved his own which were in the world, he loved them unto the horizon" (John 13:1). It was this latter expression that puzzled the boy.

As they walked home together, Ro said, "My father, that was a fine sermon . . . but there was something wrong."

"What?" Chawnga stopped and looked down at his son. No one had criticized his sermons before.

Ro continued, "You said that God's love is 'unto the horizon,' but you did not tell how far the horizon is. Tell me, how far is the horizon?"

Chawnga looked down and shook his head. He replied quietly, "I do not know."

"Is it as far away as our house?"

Again Chawnga shook his head. "I do not know, my son."

"But my father, if God loves me only as far as the horizon, as far as I can see, then he will not be with me when I am far away."

Chawnga seemed more confused than hurt or angry by the boy's argument.

"Father, how far away is the horizon?"

"I do not know," came the honest, quiet reply from his father.

Ro stated his argument in the careful, respectful Asian manner. "Father, if you talk about things you do not know, and if that is what education does for you, why then should I go to school?"

There was no answer.

But several days later, his father invited Ro to hike with him up nearby Sumtuk Mountain. When they reached the top, Chawnga said, "Let us climb this tree."

From their high perch they could see a great distance. Chawnga pointed downward.

"That is Cachar Valley, where your grandfather and other Hmars attacked the tea plantation and took five hundred heads. The smoke is from the fires that heat the tea leaves. It is many days' journey across that valley.

"Now look to the long mountain range beyond the valley. Do you see the peak where the heaven touches the earth?" He paused, waiting for Ro to respond.

"Yes, my father. Is that the horizon?"

Chawnga did not answer directly but continued, "If you were to journey many days, many weeks, you would come to the top of that mountain. But then you would look out like you are here, and you would see another mountain just like it. Then, if you were to journey more days and weeks to the second mountain, you would see a third. If you went to the third and looked, you would see yet another. My son, the horizon never ends.

"There is no place in this world where the love of God cannot reach. When you go to school, or whether you are on a mountain or in a valley, God will encircle you with his love. He will guide you, protect you, inspire you, and teach you.

"Then someday you may also be a carrier of this love that reaches to the horizon. And you may be the one to put God's Word into our language."

That vivid lesson left Ro without further argument or fear. While still in the tree with his father, he committed himself in obedience to follow God *unto the horizon.*

# Chapter Two
## *Unto the Horizon*

The important day finally came for Ro to start on his ninety-six-mile hike to the mission school in Churachandpur. His few belongings had been crammed into his small backpack.

After a hasty breakfast, Daii asked for the Lord's protection and guidance for their journey. Then, shouldering his backpack, Ro received her final, tearful embrace. Then, trying hard not to cry himself, he followed his father toward the path that led to the jungle.

Walking single file, the two of them were soon swallowed up by the thick foliage, and Ro felt another twinge of homesickness. His father sensed the problem and began pointing out the jungle sights to distract him. A black bear napped harmlessly beside a log, and two monkeys chattered and swung from the slim bamboo poles above them. Ro saw a brown turtle sunning itself on a flat rock in the river as they crossed the pole bridge. In the distance elephants trumpeted.

When they started down a long hill, Chawnga reminded Ro to carefully learn the way because Ro would have to come alone next time. Then he began to give Ro some pointers for protecting himself in the jungle.

"Suppose a big rogue elephant chases you. What would you do?"

Ro felt suddenly uncomfortable. Maybe one was lurking just ahead! "I wouldn't be able to get away. I cannot run fast enough. He would take me in his trunk and smash me against a tree."

"Oh, you would have a chance," Chawnga said with a twinkle in his eye. "You must remember that if an elephant chases you, run straight ahead. Then make a sharp turn to the right, run straight again then make another sharp turn to the right. Do this four times, and you will return to your original path."

"But how will this help me?" Ro asked.

"All elephants are left-handed and favor that side—they cannot turn quickly to the right. If elephants try, they slip and fall to the ground, and it takes them a long time to get up."

To Ro the idea sounded plausible, but he hoped he would never have to test it.

"Something else you must remember," the tribal preacher said. "Satan is left-handed, too. He is the enemy of your soul and would like nothing more than to lead a ten-year-old boy into sin. If you are tempted to do evil while you are far away from your parents, turn to the right by reading the Word of God. Tell Jesus about this rogue, and he will tumble him onto his back."

Although they saw no elephants that day, they did spot some fresh tiger tracks in the mud of a streambed. They camped for the night nestled in the shelter of a big rock cleft, and Ro fell asleep in the security of his father's prayers.

The next morning, as they walked, Chawnga began reminiscing about the Welsh missionary Watkin Roberts.

"Mr. Young Man was a very unusual white man," Chawnga recalled. "He came to India when he was just twenty-two years alive. He had been converted in a great revival among the Welsh people, and Mr. Young Man heard God calling him to go and share his faith with the people of India.

"When he came, he did not treat us the way other white men did. When we went with him by train, he would not sit in the first-class cars while we and his helpers sat in the third-class coach. No, everyone rode together. We ate together. We worshiped together.

"He made us feel important and gave us respect. He believed we were intelligent even though we did not speak his language. He tried to understand our ways, our culture.

"Mr. Young Man trained us to spread the gospel, but he did not ask us to do it in ways that are foreign. If only he could have stayed. . . ." His voice trailed off wistfully.

"Why did he leave, Father?"

"I will explain another day. When you are a bit older." Chawnga's sad expression told Ro that the story would probably not be a happy one.

They traveled and slept four more days and nights in the jungle. On the sixth day, Ro awoke stiff and sore. When he stood, a sharp pain reminded him that he had sprained his ankle the day before. There were still thirteen miles to go, four of them uphill and across Hiengkot Pass. Ro wondered if he could make it on his painful swollen foot.

After a scanty breakfast of cold rice and a little chili chutney, they started out. But Ro soon learned that every step was terrible agony. His father had made a walking stick for him, which he used as a makeshift crutch, but it was still quite hard to keep from crying out in pain from each difficult step.

Chawnga knew his son was suffering, and when the width of the trail was wide enough for them to walk side by side, he put his arm under Ro's arm, lifting and helping the boy as best as he could. Other times he used his storytelling as a diversion.

It was this interesting talk that kept Ro going until they reached the narrow Tuila River and stopped for lunch. Ro ate while cooling his burning foot in the refreshing water. Then they crossed over the river and began another uphill climb along a narrow, rocky path.

By now, Ro's foot and ankle had become painfully inflamed. His mouth was dry and his tongue began to feel like parched goatskin. Ro wondered if school could really be so important.

Hours later they reached the end of the long and painful uphill climb over the rugged mountain pass. They rested in the refreshing breeze that blew at the summit from the east.

After a short rest, Chawnga pointed out to Ro the shiny tin roofs of houses in the next valley. "It is not much farther, my son. That is Churachandpur." At last! Their destination was in sight. Ro's confidence surged, and he fairly flew down the mountainside the last couple of miles.

The two of them went directly to the mission dispensary where Chawnga spoke to a young medical practitioner, a Mr. Thanglung, and made arrangements for Ro's sprained ankle to be looked at and for his lodging.

Mr. Thanglung told Chawnga that Ro's room and board at the school would cost three rupees a month (about forty-five cents) plus "whatever work the boy is capable of doing."

The time came for Chawnga to leave. Ro clung to his father's hand, struggling to control his emotions.

"Good-bye, my son. God keep you," he said with strong self-will and glistening eyes. Then he left quickly before the boy could see his own difficulty at their parting.

The Thanglungs decided that Ro was "capable" of tending their herd of thirty-five cows. He was also "capable" of milking them twice each day. He was to rise before dawn to milk them, then take them to the fields for grazing. He would work at least four hours before his classes even started. Then, after classes, he was to go get the cows from the fields and bring them back and milk them all again—another four-hour chore *after* classes.

In Ro's "spare" time, the boy was expected to weed the garden and help with a number of household chores.

Ro envied the boys who lived in the hostel, who could play during their free time. With so much work, he had little time for study, so school-work was a struggle for him.

Despite these early difficulties, the boy's confidence began to grow. He found that some of the students had heard of his father's reputation as a fearless evangelist and strong preacher. Ro became aware that he was being looked upon as a leader because of his father.

When the students elected Ro president of a junior Christian Endeavor group, he suggested that they divide into several teams and go to witness in nearby villages. The youthful gospel teams then went out the next weekend with great enthusiasm.

Teisieng, a village six miles from the school, was totally non-Christian. The teams had tried to share their faith but returned reporting that the people were fierce in their opposition to the gospel. However, Ro knew that being the leader it was his responsibility to go and try. He had sometimes gone with his father to such a village, and he longed for his father's courage now. Ro knelt, asking God to protect him, then started out.

Even before reaching the first houses, he saw priests performing ritual sacrifices. Around them, villagers were obviously drunk and shouting to one another. Dogs were barking excitedly, and Ro's heart began pounding. He stood under a tall tree, still unnoticed but trembling. Indecision still ruled his actions, but he dropped to his knees again. "Lord, I am afraid. You gave courage to David and Joshua. Now, won't you please be with me?" he prayed.

Standing erect, Ro swallowed hard and walked straight ahead. He stopped at the first thatch house that he came to. The man inside shouted at him. "You believers of God bring nothing but trouble! Who asked you to come? Get out of here now!" Ro hastily took the hint and left.

Moving on, he stopped where three men were sitting by a fire. He walked near to them and stood quietly for a while. Finally he mustered some courage to speak. He began in the polite, respectful Asian manner. "Sirs, with your kind permission I would like to tell you a story."

"What kind of a story?" one man asked.

"It is the true story of the one true God and his Son, Jesus."

Upon hearing the name of Jesus, one of the other men jumped angrily to his feet. "Don't bother us with a dead man's story!" he cried. "Where is my *dao?*" And he reached for the long knife used for uncounted generations by the mountain people to chop bamboo, clear fields, and take heads.

Ro took to his heels as two of the men laughed and shouted obscenities after him.

But the third man started after Ro. "Wait!" he called. "Wait, I say."

The Hmar boy ran as fast as his short legs could carry him, but the villager kept gaining on him. "Don't be afraid," the man called to Ro. "I need to talk to you."

There was no malice in this man's voice, so Ro lost his fear. He stopped and waited for the man to catch up. The man smiled and said, "Someone from Churachandpur has been telling me about Jesus. I want to hear more. Will you come to my house and tell me about this Jesus?"

Though fearful of a trick, Ro went with him and shared the gospel with this stranger, using the basic structure and text from one of his father's sermons, which the boy had by now memorized.

The man listened respectfully and after an hour or so announced, "I want to give my name to Jesus." Ro was amazed.

Ro solemnly took out a piece of paper from the Lushai New Testament that he carried and wrote down the name of the first Christian from Teisieng. Then he prayed with the man, promising to return, and went back to his school rejoicing.

\*      \*      \*

November vacation time came, and Ro set out for home in the company of several older boys, who lived in various villages along the way. On their first night in the jungle they were all drenched by a cold downpour that lasted throughout the next day. At sundown they stopped at Mawngawn, an unfamiliar village, where they hoped to find shelter. It was the tribal custom to not refuse hospitality or shelter to a traveler in need.

By knocking at doors, they all found places to stay—except Ro. Dejected and soaked, the Hmar boy sat at the edge of the village, cradled his head in his lap, and began to cry.

A man's voice interrupted his sobbing. "Why are you crying?" When Ro explained, the stranger said, "I am the chief of this village. It is a shame to our village that you have found no welcome. Come. You will be my guest for the night."

The chief bent over and picked up Ro's rain-soaked backpack, and when they arrived at a large house, he asked his wife to bring dry clothes and a hot drink while a meal was prepared for Ro.

Later, he was given space on the bamboo floor to sleep, but he asked if he could move closer to the cooking fire to keep warm. As he lay there, Ro remembered the day when he climbed the big tree on top of Sumtuk Mountain. Now, he thanked God for loving him unto this horizon and fell asleep.

It took six days to walk uphill to the mission school at Churachandpur from Phulpui. But the boy was so energized by the joy of returning home, that the return trip took only four days. When Ro reached his village, he was tired but happy to be with his family again. His family now included a new baby brother whom Ro had not seen before.

Over the next several days, everyone seemed to show Ro more respect, and the maturity that came from self-sufficiency and hard work at the mission school seemed to show in the boy's self-esteem.

Ro learned that a revival was stirring in Phulpui. While it was still dark in the early morning, people rose to pray, raising their hands and praising God, asking for God's blessings upon their tribe. There were services every night, and on Sundays each unbelieving home received four or five visitors. Ro's father reported happily that God's power was exploding in other Hmar villages as well, with hundreds of tribespeople choosing to give their names to Jesus and follow on his path.

Chawnga told his son that a revival like this had followed the initial contacts of Mr. Young Man. Ro's curiosity about the Welsh missionary could not be held in check. "My father," he asked, "why did Mr. Young Man leave? Why is he not with us today?"

Chawnga looked at his growing son. His face grew sad as it had before when the boy had asked the question. This time he did not brush the question aside but sighed deeply as he spoke.

"Well, I suppose you must learn sooner or later. Sit down, and I will try to explain."

Ro sat as he was told and looked into his father's face with full attention.

"Missionaries are people like us," Chawnga began. "I have learned that some become jealous when others are successful and bring many to God. Mr. Young Man was much loved by the tribespeople. He finally obtained permission from the British agent to work in the Hmar territory. But white missionaries told the British agent that church leaders in England and America had divided up India among various groups and that because another missionary had been assigned the state of Manipur, they insisted that Mr. Young Man leave the part of Manipur where the Hmars live. So the British agent cancelled Mr. Young Man's permit."

Ro was indignant. "That was not fair!"

"Mr. Young Man then left Manipur but not India. He started a school outside the state, in his house, and we went to him there for training. Mr. Young Man believed that we, the tribal Christians, not foreign missionaries, should lead and govern our own churches. He said that we should use our own tribal songs to create music for worship and follow our own ways so long as they were pleasing to God."

"Is Mr. Young Man still in India?" Ro asked his father.

"No, my son. His missionary society was worried about the loyalty of the tribal leaders. They said we should have foreign bosses, but we did not know these people from a faraway land who wanted to rule over us. Mr. Young Man told them that they were wrong. He said, 'Even if you do not trust the natives, at least trust the Holy Spirit who operates in their hearts.' And when Mr. Young Man would not give in to their way, the mission society cut off his salary and dismissed his native workers. He was stranded in India without any money. A sympathetic Hindu gave him enough money for passage home.

"Then they sent the foreign bosses to tell us what to do. Some of our preachers refused to work for them and were whipped publicly by officials. I was also beaten and put in jail for not following their commands."

Chawnga saw Ro's expression turn serious. He quickly told the boy, "Do not let this worry you, my son. We are not responsible for the mistakes and sins of others. Remember, most missionaries are doing good. Without them, there would be no school in Churachandpur for you to attend."

"Yes, I know," Ro agreed. "But does Mr. Young Man yet live?"

Chawnga nodded. "He lives far across the ocean in a land called Canada. He works hard to raise money for India. Some of us still receive letters from him. He hopes to one day come back, but his health is not good."

"If he comes back," said Ro, "I will be the one to carry his luggage all over the hills."

\*       \*       \*

The two months of Ro's school vacation passed all too quickly, and he had to return to Churachandpur once more. This time he went alone; his father did not accompany him.

By day it was not so bad. But at night the fears and sounds of the jungle haunted him enormously.

One night Ro was awakened by the throaty growl of a tiger. He knew it was hopeless to run. A Royal Bengal tiger could easily outrun and catch him. He could only lie very still under the tree, listening, as the jungle cat circled ever closer until he could determine that the tiger was

29

within springing distance. What was there to do but pray?

"Lord, I do not want to be this tiger's breakfast," he prayed succinctly. "Please keep his mouth shut and send him away!"

Just then he saw the tiger! It stood up in the tall grass and started walking away—just as he had asked God. Ro held his breath and watched as the beast withdrew from view. He listened to the swish of the grass until the sound became fainter and fainter. Sure that the tiger had finally disappeared into the jungle, Ro finally took a breath. Then he thanked God for once again loving him unto this horizon.

School was more enjoyable for Ro the second year. He did well in all his subjects except English. Unfortunately, his teachers had learned English from other Indians for the most part, and each person accented and pronounced the words quite differently. It was all very confusing. Not only were the English words hard to pronounce, there were so many exceptions to the grammatical and spelling rules.

Despite his difficulties with English, Ro liked his other subjects. He was especially fond of geography and liked to imagine going to all the new places he had learned about.

He traced on a map of the world just how far Watkin Roberts—Mr. Young Man—had traveled from his homeland of Wales to bring the gospel to the hill people of northeast India. Then he traced his finger across the great Pacific Ocean along a route that he thought American missionaries might have used to come to India.

These fascinating lands on the other side of the world particularly intrigued him. *What wonders are there?* he thought. He had heard of stories brought back by tribesmen, who had been taken by the British to fight in the great war nearly a quarter century earlier. He heard such men tell of eating meals out of "iron gourds," of seeing a machine that flew like a great bird, and of visiting a place where steel "vines" grew on tall tree trunks planted alongside the roads. These somehow allowed men to hear the words of other men in far-off places by talking into a strange device and listening to the words come back.

And there were other tales, many of them embellished over the years. Ro wished that he might one day go see these things for himself.

The year Ro turned twelve, he reminded his father of a secret wish. Chawnga was leaving for an eighty-mile walk to a trading post to buy supplies. "My father," the boy pleaded, "if you could, if it is possible, I would like a pair of shoes."

At the time Chawnga made no promises, but he returned many days later with a pair of white sneakers. Ro slipped them on his feet; they looked wonderful. He took them off, then tried them on again. On and off, on and off again. He felt like royalty.

Running to proudly show his friends, Ro accidentally stepped in some wet mud. His beautiful shoes were completely soiled! Sadly, he hurried home, washed off the red clay, and put the sneakers by the stove to dry.

Two hours later Ro was horrified to see that the rubber had melted away from the soles. When he tried them on again, his toes stuck out. How he cried, berating himself. Early the next morning he sought out Chawnga. "I know that you spent

31

much money, my father. I am deeply sorry for my foolishness. Can you forgive me?"

"My son," Chawnga replied kindly, "I will always have as much forgiveness as you need. Let us pray about it."

Looking heavenward, his father talked to God. "Lord, because of his ignorance, my son has ruined his first pair of shoes. Will you forgive him? I have already done so."

And that quickly settled the matter.

\*     \*     \*

Forgiveness was something that interested Ro, and he thought of the concept many times as he studied history the next year. So many lessons seemed to be about wars and killing. His own people had fought in the Great War (World War I) in Europe.

Now stories were coming that another war in Europe had started up, led by an "evil chief," Hitler.

Ro, now fifteen, had finished his primary schooling when the Japanese invaded the subcontinent. They landed first in Rangoon, Burma, then began marching into India.

Ro had planned to attend the American Baptist High School in Jorhat, Assam, some three hundred miles from Phulpui. But now word had come that the Japanese were advancing north from nearby Burma to that area.

The British had brought in Allied troops and were occupying the Jorhat school, which had become the barracks for prisoners of war.

Fired by patriotic fervor, Ro tried hard to enlist in the Indian army. Age was not a problem—the Hmars kept no birth records. But the Indian army regulations said a recruit must be at least sixty inches tall and have a thirty-three-inch chest.

At fifteen, he was tall enough. Still, no matter how deep a breath he took, Ro couldn't make his chest swell enough to pass.

Although he didn't qualify as a soldier, Ro still wanted to help. The Japanese were moving ever farther into the tribal lands and closer than ever to their homes.

Allied general "Vinegar Joe" Stillwell visited the war front at Imphal. The Japanese were within striking distance of Imphal and in a matter of days would overrun that city.

The Allied general determined that his troops, unfamiliar with the mountains and jungle terrain, could not adequately infiltrate the vast area of Japanese occupation to gather intelligence on troop movements and locations. So he began to recruit loyal Indians to become "intelligence informants."

One day an army man told Ro that, although he couldn't be a soldier, he could be an informant for Allied Intelligence.

"You mean a *spy?*" he asked.

"Yes, in a way. You can report enemy troop locations. Track their movements, and you can help rescue downed pilots or other Allied military men."

A "bamboo telegraph" was set up all across the jungles that passed the word along about Japanese movements and activities. Ro was proud to be serving his country as a link in that system.

# Chapter Three
## *Japanese Invasion*

The hill people fled from the iron monsters that clanked through the villages, spewing fire and thunder. The people ran in terror when giant shiny birds with markings of the rising sun roared overhead, and they looked for places to hide in order to escape the great killing explosions called bombs.

The invaders nearly overran Imphal, capital of the state of Manipur. Everywhere else, jungle travel was really unsafe. After running into two armed Japanese patrols, Chawnga decided he had to curtail his tours of preaching and watch over his family.

Still, despite their fears, the tribal people helped the Allied cause. Their communications network of runners used hollowed-out bamboo to carry letters and Allied communiqués despite knowing that if any of them were caught, it was likely that they would be shot on the spot.

Ro belonged to this ragtag force of brave intelligence couriers. He spied out the hidden Japanese troop locations and coordinated these hideouts for the Allied army.

His most appreciated accomplishment was when he discovered the command post of the Japanese warlord, General Sato. In order to get as much information as possible, Ro knew he had to get inside the command post area. This was risky. Informants and spies were quickly executed if discovered. But since he was just fifteen (and looked younger), Ro felt he could take the risk.

He gathered several *daos* (machete-style knives), packed them inside an old bag, and approached the camp. A guard raised his rifle at the young man and shouted in Japanese. Using the few words of Japanese he had learned, Ro showed the soldier his knives and demonstrated how well they worked at clearing jungle growth.

As the Japanese soldiers tried out his wares, Ro looked around the command post and made mental notes of the surroundings.

When he later reported to the Allied command, British dive-bombers were called up. They flew in over Imphal and bombed and strafed General Sato's command post. The raid destroyed the outpost causing the Japanese to retreat to the Burma border, and they never returned.

Ro was paid for his intelligence reports either in money—or in a much more valuable trading commodity—cigarettes, which he could sell for even more money.

That gave Ro an idea. As a trader traveling through the mountains, he'd have an excellent excuse for going to and from the various villages and being near the front lines.

"I can scout for the Allied forces and also earn money for my education," Ro told his father. He was so convincing that Chawnga loaned him one hundred rupees to get started.

Ro bought supplies of mountain-grown chilies, which he carried on his back for four days, selling them at a profit in the valley. Then he purchased a basket of assorted knives, razor blades, cotton yarn, needles, and thread, along with assorted medicines and vitamins to peddle in villages near the front lines. It was also the best way for a "harmless" tribal boy to gather intelligence.

The war brought not only destruction to the villages but also soaring prices for any goods. Survivors were paid for providing even the most ordinary of services—many of them were hired as porters, cooks, aides, or translators. Others whose farms escaped the ravages had home-grown produce that they could sell.

Ro bought from them and sold to them as well. They were eager for store-bought items that Ro supplied, especially items like aspirin and vitamins, along with very valuable cholera or malaria tablets.

Japanese patrols had gone through village after village, killing and being killed, leaving unburied, decaying corpses across the landscape. As a horrible result, dysentery and cholera were spreading.

In Ro's first visit to the area, he found a friendly but needy people. In his basket was a bottle of five hundred cholera pills that he had bought for twenty rupees. Because of the need, he thought of asking one rupee for five pills. That would give him a good profit and not be too expensive for his customers.

But in the village of Bualtang, high on a Manipur hillside, Ro learned an interesting bit of economic psychology. At his first stop, he described how the pills would stop "running stomachs." Then he overheard a listener nearby comment, "Too cheap to do good work. Last month I bought one tablet that cost me two rupees, so when I swallowed it, I knew that it had to be good medicine!"

Taking the hint, Ro moved to another part of the village and began selling pills for one rupee each. By the next morning, he had sold all five hundred tablets and left the village with a profit of 430 rupees.

As the war turned against Japan, the invaders became more fierce. It was becoming more dangerous for the intelligence runners to travel through the mountains. Ro felt it was best to settle down for a while and farm. He had little experience but was willing to work hard and made plans to find a plot of land.

Each year sites from the communally owned land were apportioned among the farmers. They drew lots for the locations and sizes of their plots, leaving latecomers with the least desirable lots. Because Ro had made his decision late, he got a site on the main path connecting two villages through which pigs and cattle were driven daily.

Ro bought an axe and a long, sharp *dao* to clear the jungle trees and thick undergrowth. Then he went to work with great gusto, first chopping, then hacking, finally dragging brush into piles for burning.

Initially, this strenuous exercise was exhilarating. Then it became work. After that, pure misery. All his time on those difficult trails hadn't conditioned Ro for such work. Muscles ached, and the axe was heavy as a log in his hands. Painful blisters popped up on his palms, and in a short time they broke open and bled. His enthusiasm wore thin, and Ro wanted to quit, to find an easier way to earn money for his education. Yet he was disciplined, so he kept at it.

Each night after dark, he dragged himself home from his *jhum* (farm). Dawn came all too quickly and the torturous cycle started all over.

After nearly a month, Ro had finally cleared the land. Then, like the other farmers, he recuperated while the brush dried in order to be burned.

The Hmars had a time for everything. Cotton and sesame seed were to be sown when the *bung* tree blossomed. Soybeans were planted a month later when the cicadas sang. Rice was dropped into the ground five lunar months after the last harvest.

Ro found that planting was much faster than clearing the jungle, but the ashes left after burning the brush made the job messy, especially after rains.

In the field, Ro had no shade to shield him from the sun's scorching rays, and he got severe sunburn on his back.

Finally the first green shoots brought a sense of accomplishment and encouragement. But Ro already knew that plans for his lifework did not include farming. Yet, he did his best, going to the field every day, including Saturdays. He pulled weeds, piled them, then carried them to a pile outside the plot. He packed extra soil around each rice plant. These were things his neighbors did not do, but Ro kept at it diligently.

Summer mellowed into autumn and then harvesttime, the climax of a year's hard work. Ro had 160 bushels of rice! No one had expected him to have so many. A neighboring farmer with far more land had harvested only half as much. Ro thanked God for the bounty and set aside 16 bushels as a tithe.

*     *     *

The war slowly ground to an end, and at last the Japanese announced their surrender. Now, more than ever, Ro wanted to continue his education. He had saved his money from trading and farming to pay for his first year of high school, but where would he go? And if he completed high school, what about college?

Ro heard that some American GIs were taking Indian young men back with them to the United States, where an education was supposed to be easier to get. This sounded like a fantastic opportunity. He walked five days to Cachar, then took a train to the enormous city of Calcutta, accompanied by two Hmar businessmen.

So sure was he that he'd be picked by an American GI to go with him to the United States that Ro said good-bye to his Hmar companions and went to the recruiting center.

He found out where the American recruiter was interviewing those who wanted to come to the U.S., but Ro could not understand anything he said. Americans who spoke English did not speak it with the same accent as the British, and the British did not say the words the same as Indians.

He was able to determine for himself that the procedure was to stand in line and wait for someone to choose you. This he did. He stood in line all day, but no one picked him. How he wished his English were better. After two days of being overlooked, it became apparent that Ro was not going to America.

He was dejected. The trip to Calcutta had used up most of his savings. Yet, since he had traveled all this way, he thought he'd try to enroll at the Salvation Army Officer Training School in Calcutta. Surely he would learn English this way.

He found the address and talked to the admissions director, who turned him down. "Our minimum age is twenty. Come back in five years—and work on learning English. Your Eng- lish is not good," the Salvation Army man told him plainly.

English had been his weakest subject in school, but he hoped it would not keep him from finding a high school to take him. Yet, that's exactly what happened.

Three more Calcutta schools turned him down, and since he had no more leads, Ro returned home dejected.

Chawnga and Daii welcomed him with open arms, and he poured out his sorrows to them. His parents did not seem as sad as he was. Daii said, "We prayed and asked God to save you from going to America, so you could go to a high school in India and someday translate the Bible for our people."

Then Chawnga reminded Ro of his opportunity based on the commitment of his older brother. "You know that according to our tribal customs, Ramlien, our oldest son, will receive the inheritance—along with the responsibility of caring for us in our old age.

"But you are free to get the education that will fit you for the task of translating the Bible for our people who need it so badly. We know that with God's help you can do it."

Ro swallowed hard and looked at his parents. They had such great expectations for him. It seemed that, instead of being defeated by this recent bitter failure, he was being guided by the Lord toward a higher calling.

After reflecting for several moments, Ro said with quiet determination, "My dear mother and father, I *will* go to school and be the one to translate the Bible for the Hmar people."

# Chapter Four
## *Your Head Will Be Cut Off!*

Still eager to start high school, Ro found a school in the hill village of Lungthulien, in Manipur, set up as a temporary facility to meet the emergency situation created by the war, by his old friend Mr. Thanglung, the man with whom he had boarded at Churachandpur.

The school year was half over when Ro came to meet with Mr. Thanglung, who greeted him warmly but cautioned, "You will be wasting your money. You've already missed half of your classes. You cannot possibly make up this time and pass the year-end examinations in November. Rochunga, if I were you, I would pack my bags and go home and wait until next year."

But Ro was determined. "I would rather try and fail, sir, than not try at all." His mind was made up, so he paid his tuition and began classes the next day.

To further complicate the tribal boy's life, there was no dorm, so Ro bargained with a local family to make arrangements to let him stay with them in the village. Ro agreed to give his services doing chores in exchange for room and board.

The place they gave him was a corner of their large one-room bamboo house. Despite the choking smoke that always seemed to bellow from the fireplace at one end of the room, there was little actual heat from its fire. Not only that, there was hardly room for Ro to spread his bedroll in the space assigned to him because the family was also boarding four other students.

Living with these other students, along with the large family, made study difficult. A steady stream of visitors made concentration nearly impossible. Ro's solution was to build himself a shelter in a tree in the nearby jungle. When heavy rain and darkness drove him from this haven, he took his books to the tiny back porch and read aloud to drown out the noise from inside the house.

Week after week Ro studied diligently. With only one teacher, who himself had just a high school education, many of his questions went unanswered. For the most part Ro had to learn on his own. He memorized most of the geometry textbook, both theorems and problems, without instruction.

But it was not all drudgery. He was asked to teach a Sunday school class at the church in Lungthulien and occasionally he took time out for hunting and fishing.

Ro went to the nearby Tuibum River and watched as tribal fishermen taught him a new way to fish. When they saw rain clouds gather on the mountaintops they built a dam in the river. A man told Ro that the gathering rainwater would come downriver in two days, and they must be ready. Then they built a reed and bamboo funnel-like device that emptied the water into a small dug-out lagoon beside the flowing river.

When the river was swollen with rainwater two days later, the dam had forced the fish into the large funnel. Then fishermen "herded" them into the small lagoon and from there into the cooking pots.

On Saturdays Ro left the school grounds and went to the forest for three or four hours to set his *be-ai* (pheasant snares) which resulted in having fine meat on the table to go with the rice.

November came. It was time for the final school examinations to determine if he would get credit for a year's work. Ro had tried his very best; now he could only trust God to help him recall what he had studied.

When the results were announced, he learned that he had finished fourth in a class of twenty-eight! He hurried to the church and offered a prayer of thanksgiving to the Lord.

The next day, Ro prepared for the long journey back home. He took a sampan down the river part of the way; then he started a two-day trek over a narrow trail where for a mile or two the riverbank itself was the only path. Walking near the river, he saw some fresh footprints of a deer. Then, he saw a footprint of a tiger, as well as a tiger stool that was still steaming. The Royal Bengal had to be close by and may even have scented him.

Ro decided to go on anyway, thinking that the tiger might more readily attack if he were retreating than bravely advancing. As he walked along he saw more footprints. Ro judged the tiger to be a six-footer, quite a big fellow.

Then, after the trail left the river, he heard a noise about a hundred yards to his left. Looking that way, he glimpsed a reddish streak through a break in the underbrush.

There was no turning back now, so Ro continued slowly, making no sudden moves. He could still see the tall grass moving as the tiger seemed to be moving parallel to him. Once he turned his eyes and even caught a glimpse of the huge cat. Ro prayed silently and kept walking.

After five miles of walking with the tiger stalking him, he neared the village. As soon as he got closer and heard the noise of human activity, the tiger turned back. Ro felt as if the Lord must have sent that tiger for a purpose. *Perhaps there was some greater danger in the jungle, and God sent the tiger as sort of a bodyguard,* he thought. *Certainly no other jungle animal or even robbers would attack me if they knew the tiger was there.*

"Thank you, Lord, for your protection," he said aloud.

Chawnga and Daii were pleased to hear of their industrious son's achievement in finishing a year's schoolwork in half the time. Daii had grown some red-hot chilies in her garden and was drying them for Ro to sell.

Ro suggested that he carry the chilies down the mountain to Lakhipur, a four-day journey. It was much farther away than the usual market, but he could sell them for a higher profit.

So Ro struck out for the valley with a heavy load of sixty pounds of chilies yoked to his back. He sold them and used the double profit to buy merchandise to sell in the small villages on his way back. By Christmas, he'd earned enough to cover the expenses of his next year of high school.

He left for the American Baptist High School in Jorhat, Assam, some three hundred miles away, in January, 1946. This was the first time he had taken such a long train trip by himself.

En route, he apparently did not hear the conductor tell about the need to change trains at a certain station halfway to Jorhat. He was left stranded at the station. He went inside the train station to get out of the hot sun.

At dusk the stationmaster chased him outside to wait for the next day's train.

Ro walked to a small grassy area under some trees and sat down. It was dark and cold and in a very remote area. Not long after he sat down under the trees, he heard some loud shouting and men coming his way. It was a gang of unruly Naga tribesmen. Several seemed drunk and belligerent. They were quite intimidating with jungle garb and large grotesque tattoos. Ro felt his pulse quicken and hoped they wouldn't see him. He ducked into the shadows.

They kept up their loud and boisterous activity, and it was apparent that it would go on all night. Ro knew that he was out of place here in their territory. If they discovered him, they would likely rob and beat him—or worse, *kill* him.

Suddenly, amidst the din of their shouts, Ro thought he heard something else. He strained to hear it. Then, the sound became clearer. It was a flute. Its plaintive notes seemed to rise above the din. Ro recognized the tune and the familiar words resounded in his head, *What a friend we have in Jesus, all our sins and griefs to bear!*

Ro prayed that the music would continue as he got up and tried to locate its source. He rushed through the trees and climbed over a fence. It was dark, and the ground was unfamiliar, but he kept walking toward the sound of the flute. *Have we trials and temptations? Is there trouble anywhere? We should never be discouraged, take it to the Lord in prayer.*

He was getting closer to the sound of the flute. Climbing over another fence in the darkness, he came to a house. Sitting on the porch was a man wearing a shirt and cap that identified him as a railway employee.

As Ro came close, the man didn't see him at first, but continued playing. The words again echoed in Ro's mind, *Are we weak and heavy laden, 'cumbered with a load of care? Precious Savior, still our refuge; take it to the Lord in prayer.*

The man stopped playing when Ro stood before him. Ro smiled and greeted him in Hmar. The man replied in Naga. Neither man understood the other, but Ro gestured, putting his hand across his heart, saying, "Christian. Christian."

The Naga man understood immediately. His face brightened. He put his hand on his own heart. "Christian." He smiled broadly.

To the Naga, the universally understood *Christian* meant fellowship. He gestured to Ro to come with him and took him into his small house. He prepared some food to share with Ro.

After Ro had eaten, he sang some hymns as the man played his flute. Although they could not communicate in words, each shared the love that God had placed in their hearts.

Ro was given shelter and a place to sleep by the gentle Naga man, and in the morning he escorted Ro to the station to catch his train to Jorhat.

Despite the delay over the train mix-up, Ro still arrived at the American Baptist High School in Jorhat a full two weeks before the semester began. Upon his arrival he asked the one resident missionary for a job.

Miss Johnstone took him to a massive mound of dirt, the result of trenches dug during the war, that ran the full perimeter of the mission compound, nearly three blocks in length.

Miss Johnstone told him bluntly, "You can fill in these trenches around the compound. Now that the war's over, they aren't needed anymore."

Ro offered to contract for the job in the tribal way, being paid for each trench that he filled. But Miss Johnstone insisted that he work by the hour. "And any time not spent working will be deducted from your pay," she warned him.

The next morning after eating breakfast Ro, attacked the mountains of dirt. He filled a big basket that he carried on his head a quarter-mile to dump into the trench. It was most exhausting work, and Ro was almost ready to give up by noon.

Yet, if he stopped working, he would not be paid for the day, and although working by the hour was so much more tiring than his "by the job" method, Ro kept at it, day after grueling day, from dawn to dark.

At the end of two weeks, the mountain of dirt was gone, and eight trenches were filled. Ro received his pay—just enough to pay for his meals for the two-week period he had already worked!

When his classes began, he accepted another job—that of dorm sweeper. This menial task held the lowest status in India, but he needed the work. Before sweeping, Ro had to walk a half mile to get water to sprinkle on the dirt floors. Then he spent up to two hours each day sweeping and cleaning. It was a frustrating job, since many of the students wore World War II surplus army combat boots that kicked up much more dirt, but at least this was a contract job. He was paid about three cents a day.

Ro did well in all classes except one. Not surprisingly, English was still his downfall. And what he had learned at Churachandpur was more a hindrance than help. He thought *whole* was pronounced "hool" and that *floor* was "floer" — since, after all, *door* was pronounced "doer" by other tribals who learned English.

There were so many strange variations that had no logic. For example, *threw* and *through* were pronounced identically but had different spellings and meanings. And *bow* and *bough* caused the same problem. Except that *bow* could mean to bend oneself in respect or an implement used with arrows, depending on how the *o* was pronounced.

And you couldn't learn English by memorizing pronunciation. Why in the world, Ro wondered, should *laugh* and *calf* sound the same when they are spelled so differently?

One problem was that he had been taught English by people who really couldn't speak the language themselves. He took the dictionary and tried memorizing words. But try as he would, he kept tangling up sentence structure.

English was quite different from his mother tongue. In the Hmar language there are no masculine and feminine pronouns, so it was a common slip to talk about a man as "she" or a woman as "he." And the noun always comes before the predicate. Ro kept wanting to say, "Rice, did you eat it?" instead of asking, "Did you eat your rice?"

Also, in Hmar the adjectives are placed differently. He would say, "the dress, pretty and red" and not "the pretty red dress."

He struggled with English until his brain seemed to ache. He tried using English at every opportunity, but his tongue kept stumbling. He knew he had no chance of going to college without mastering English, yet he feared he would never learn.

The missionary and national teachers at the Jorhat school put great emphasis on knowing English, which they hoped would become a common unifying tongue to the twenty different language groups attending the high school. The prayer meetings that convened each evening were always conducted in this terrible foreign language called English.

Ro looked forward to these meetings with mixed feelings. He enjoyed the times of worship, singing, and prayer but lived in dread of being called upon to lead in prayer and having to use his ragged English.

That time finally came. He rose, trembling. For a while no words came to him. Then he began hesitantly, "Our heavenly Father. . . ." But he couldn't think of another English word to follow. He stood there in an embarrassed silence, grabbing the back of the pew in front of him. His knees were knocking so hard that his hands on the pew shook, making several friends giggle. Then, after what seemed to Ro to be an eternity of this tortured silence, the leader pronounced a loud "Amen."

Ro slumped in the rough wooden pew, utterly humiliated and frustrated. The prayer service was dismissed, and he ran to his dorm.

Irang Marak, his dorm "father," came to his bunk to see what was wrong. "Are you sick?" he asked.

Ro whispered, "A little. . . ."

Then Irang put his hand on Ro's head and prayed, "Lord, help this boy. He needs to know English. Help him. In Jesus' name we pray, amen."

When Irang left, Ro continued to pray. "Lord, have you forsaken me? How can I learn if I do not know how to speak English? Why can I not learn it?"

He considered packing his bags and giving up, even leaving in the middle of the night to avoid further humiliation by the other students over his trouble with English. But while kneeling, a voice seemed to say, *I love you, Rochunga. You must stay here. I will be with you and help you. I have still more things to teach you. Do you not remember that I have promised to be with you unto the horizon?*

A wonderful calmness swept over him, and Ro knew that he would stick to the task of learning English; he would keep trying.

After finishing his sweeping chores the next morning, he walked over to the mission bungalow and borrowed the English language version of the *Book of Common Prayer* and *A Book of Prayers for the Armed Forces*. Within two weeks he had memorized every prayer in the two books. Miraculously, the English language, which had been a mystery to him for so long, now began to unfold for him. He had gone to exactly the right source for victory.

Near the end of Ro's first year at Jorhat, its principal, Dr. J. W. Cook, returned from furlough in his home town of Herman, Minnesota, in America. This big, humble, spiritual man helped change the distorted stereotype that Ro had of missionaries. Except for the legendary Watkin Roberts (Mr. Young Man), whom he had never seen, Ro thought that all white missionaries lived in luxurious, comfortable bungalows with many native servants. Missionaries were perceived as taking long naps each afternoon, then strolling leisurely about each evening, doing no work except for preaching weekly sermons.

But Dr. Cook was always busy. He taught, preached, wrote, sang, visited, prayed, played, did repairs, painted the house, mowed the lawn—everything. Yet, somehow this missionary was always available as a friendly and kind surrogate parent for the students. Ro loved this huge, affable headmaster.

During this time the word of what was happening in other parts of India began to trickle into Assam. Mahatma Gandhi, the popular Hindu reformer and spokesman for independence, rose in prominence after World War II ended.

For the first time Ro was being introduced to the ideas of India's Freedom Fighters. One of them he knew well. H. K. Bawichhuaka was the first Hmar tribesman to join the Freedom Fighters' movement. He fought the British, was arrested, then imprisoned in Jorhat by the British colonial government.

Bawichhuaka was older than Ro, but they shared a common heritage. Both of their fathers had been converted to Christianity by missionary Roberts. Dohnuna, the father of Bawichhuaka, had been a successful businessman who left his trade to work with Roberts. When Roberts was forced to leave India, he had entrusted the work of the growing churches to Dohnuna. Roberts called Dohnuna "my only brother."

Just like Chawnga, Ro's father, Dohnuna was also beaten and jailed for disobeying the British missionaries and colonial missionary "bosses" in matters of faith. "But God is our master," Dohnuna and Chawnga would tell the persecutors.

Once when he was severely threatened by British and American mission leaders, Dohnuna cabled Watkin Roberts, now in Toronto:

WALKER, ROSTAD, AND COLEMAN ARE
THREATENING AND ASK ME TO GO TO AIJAL
FOR THE SAKE OF MY WIFE AND CHILDREN
BUT I HAVE REFUSED FOR CALVARY'S SAKE.

(Walker was the British District Magistrate and the other two men were American missionaries.)

Dohnuna's son, Bawichhuaka, had the same sense of resolve and character. Ro visited the Freedom Fighter many times while he was in prison. Ro also brought him books and writing materials. It was here in prison, Ro learned later, that Bawichhuaka wrote many laws for the new government of Mizoram after India later gained its independence.

Ro's view of missionaries brightened during his second year at the American Baptist high school. Plagued by dysentery, he was twice admitted to the mission hospital, for a month each time. The dehydrating effects of dysentery resulted in death for many tribespeople, so Ro was naturally anxious about the illness. But a missionary couple, Dr. and Mrs. Frank Curry, prepared special meals in their home for the Hmar young man, using fewer spices and oils. The nutritious and less irritating food, along with their tender loving care, worked. Ro regained his health and vigor and returned to school.

Meanwhile, in India, the British now offered the people independence and liberty, provided the Hindu-dominated Congress Party and the Muslim League could reach a settlement. The decision was finally made, after much debate and bloodshed, to partition Britain's largest colony into two independent nations. The Hindu majority would be called India, and the Muslim-dominated areas were to become East and West Pakistan.

Independence Day in India, August 15, 1947, was wildly celebrated at Ro's high school in Jorhat. As students listened to Nehru speak to them by radio, they jumped and shouted for joy. The new prime minister appealed for peace and order. "The British ruled us yesterday, but today is in our hands. Our maturity as a nation will be demonstrated by the way we treat our British guests."

Back in Ro's Hmar area, there was another reason for celebrating—the old British edict that had severely restricted religious freedom of the Hmar Christians by keeping them under the tight supervision of various Western overseas mission organizations was now lifted.

The tribal peoples were generally either pagan animists or Christians. Thus, they did not have to experience the bloody religious riots that were convulsing other areas.

Hindus and Muslims were either jockeying for control or fleeing to the safety of their respective majorities. Gandhi, a Hindu, was assassinated by one of his own while trying to bring peace in Bengal. Had Gandhi's killer been a Muslim instead of a Hindu fanatic, the bloodbath of revenge would have been horrific.

Upon returning for his senior year at the American Baptist High School in Jorhat, Ro was appointed the "Cleanliness Supervisor" by Dr. Cook. Instead of just sweeping floors, Ro was responsible for seeing that the dorm and dining room were kept clean at all times in an effort to prevent dysentery.

Despite an impressive title, the job was not enjoyable, nor did the students always appreciate his reminders to clean up their rooms and the dining hall.

Some complained that this was Ro's job, after all, and he should do it for "all the money" he was being paid—about four cents a day "just for walking around" with a paper and pencil, noting what needed to be done. Chuba, a non-Christian from the Ao Naga tribe, especially resented Ro. The brawny, short-tempered soccer player deliberately smeared rice and crumbs onto the table after each meal.

Ro explained to the students how such a mess attracted flies, which in turn spread diarrhea and dysentery. He asked them all to cooperate, but Chuba continued to make messes in the dining hall.

The other sweepers complained to Ro about the extra work caused by Chuba's littering. So Ro approached the strapping athlete at the next meal and asked him politely, "Are you the one who is making the mess?"

Chuba jumped up defiantly and pushed his chest into Ro's face. "Yes! I am the one!" he declared arrogantly. "And what will you do about it? Nothing! Because you are nothing. *Sala!*" He emphasized the last word, using an Assamese expression of utter contempt.

Ro did not back down. "Well, the sweepers refuse to clean up your mess. You had better clean it up yourself, or I will have to report you to Dr. Cook," he said, drawing himself up to his full five-foot-two-inch height.

"Report *me!?*" the Ao Naga exploded. "If you do, I will *kill you!* Do you understand me? I will *kill* you!" he threatened Ro, following it with a barrage of obscenities.

A crowd began to gather. Other Ao Naga students spoke to each other in their own dialect, which Ro did not understand. Then suddenly they started shouting and jeering, joining in the abuse. They began moving as a small mob toward Ro when a friend grabbed him and ushered him out of the dining hall and to his room.

That evening more than fifty Ao Naga students were absent from the scheduled prayer meeting. Ro was there, but when he returned to his room, a scrawled sign was tacked to his door announcing: "Rochunga, tonight your head will be cut off!"

Above the words of the threat was a crude but explicit drawing of a human head and a long Naga *dao.*

Several students watched as Ro took the sign down and carried it with him inside his room. Placing it on the bed, he knelt and prayed, "Lord, what shall I do? I am afraid that they mean to do this. They would lose face if they backed down after announcing this to everyone. What shall I do, Lord?"

A voice spoke to Ro's heart. *Trust in me. You need only my protection. You are safely in my hand.*

A few minutes later several of Ro's friends from Manipur were crowding into his room. The tribal students, many of whom were only one generation from head-hunting, were choosing sides. The air was tense.

"We also have *daos,*" one of his friends said. "Let's ambush them. Half will be dead before they know what happened!"

"No," Ro replied calmly. "Eight cannot win against fifty. Besides, God will not have us show them his love by killing them."

"Well, at least let us stay with you in your room tonight so we can protect you," another insisted.

"No," Ro answered. "That would break the dorm rules. But before you leave, I would like you to join me in prayer."

The students from Manipur stood by Ro as he prayed, asking God to work in the hearts of the Ao Naga young men, that the Lord would touch their lives, that peace would prevail. Then his friends left.

It was well after midnight when Ro lay down to sleep. He could feel his heart racing, and his chest was wet with sweat.

He thought about the door to his dormitory room, which had no lock. A stray dog barked noisily in a nearby field. The moon rose in the east, casting a faint light across the room.

Understandably restless and unable to sleep, Ro got up, lit a candle, opened his New Testament at random, and sat down on the edge of his bed. He began to read:

I count all things but loss for the excellency of the knowledge of Christ

Jesus my Lord: for whom I have suffered
the loss of all things, and do count them
but dung, that I may win Christ,

And be found in him, not having mine
own righteousness, which is of the law,
but that which is through the faith of
Christ, the righteousness which is of God
by faith: That I may know him, and the
power of his resurrection, and the
fellowship of his sufferings, being made
conformable unto his death; if by any
means I might attain unto the resurrection of the dead.

—Philippians 3:8-11

As he read, two phrases leaped from the
page: "the power of his resurrection" and "the
resurrection of the dead." Once again he prayed,
"Lord, if the Ao Nagas are going to cut off my
head, let them do it swiftly and completely. Don't
let them just seriously wound me. But if you are
going to protect me, please give me sleep."

He lay down again, and within seconds fell
into a deep slumber. The next morning he awoke
fully refreshed.

A Lotha Naga boy came to him. He shared
the room with Ro and must have feared whether
the Ao Nagas would be able to tell the difference
between him and Ro in the dark. He had placed
his bed against the door so they would have to
force the door and move the bed in order to get in.

He said to Ro, "They will not come now. It
is daylight. I was up all night, and I heard them
come and then go back. More than once they tried
the door. But they always went back. They could

have gotten in. My bed in front of the door would not have kept them out."

"God kept us safe," Ro replied simply.

His roommate asked, "Did you really sleep? Were you not afraid?"

Ro shook his head. "Not really. Jesus gave me peace and watched over me."

Dr. Cook was looking for Ro. "I received a report of the incident in the dining room last evening," he said. Then he asked what had happened. Ro explained, and Dr. Cook asked Ro to come to his bungalow, where both knelt down and prayed. Dr. Cook implored, "Lord, give us victory! Lord, give us victory!" Later he called in the Ao Naga student leaders. They spent long hours talking. Two days later, three of the leaders, including Chuba, came to Ro at the close of prayer meeting.

Chuba confessed, "We went to your room several times that night. We had sharp *daos* and truly intended to take your head."

Fear filled his eyes as Chuba continued. "But every time we got close to your room, something stopped us. It was like an invisible wall was there, and we could not pass through it. Each time, we tried to go into the room, but we were forced to go back!"

The hair on Ro's neck stood up, for he realized it was God who had delivered him.

Amazed, Chuba was quite repentant. He was not at all concerned about "saving face" with the other students. He and the other student leaders broke down and wept, asking for Ro's forgiveness.

Forgiveness was extended, and the young men prayed together. After that, Ro was humbled by the manifestation of "the power of his resurrection," and his heart was filled with love for these young men.

Soon after this experience, life at the high school began to settle down. In all, Ro spent three and a half years at the school, including summer and winter holidays and vacations. During these times, Ro was all alone, and he experienced extreme loneliness. All the buildings were empty; he had no one with whom he could talk. At night the only sounds were the sounds of jackals howling in the nearby jungle.

Ro thought about earning money so he could go home during the summer vacation. As he wondered how he could find such work, rains had already begun high in the nearby mountains. The normally shallow creeks soon would carry the rising waters into the narrow Toklai River. This river flowed right through the Jorhat school grounds; in fact, it separated the buildings—the school and the student dormitories on one side of the river and the church and mission offices on the other. The British had built a bridge over the river during World War II, when the school housed hundreds of prisoners of war.

A sudden flash flood had eroded many of the creeks and washed the debris into the river. Now it was swollen with dead logs and even huge uprooted trees. Several of these trees and branches had caught on the pilings of the bridge. If something was not done, the entire bridge would be in danger of giving way.

Dr. Cook came out in the morning to inspect the bridge. It was creaking and groaning at the stress. Every now and then another huge log would smash into the pilings with such force that it was too dangerous to be on the bridge. Dr. Cook called the students and asked for volunteers to help clear the debris.

But none of the boys had enough confidence in his swimming skills to dare to battle that fearful current, fearing that anyone who tried would be swept underwater or struck with a log. There were all kinds of ways to die in the process of trying to clear the debris. No one volunteered.

But if something was not done right away, it would be hopeless, and the mission would lose an important and strategic bridge.

At this point, the Bible teacher, Rev. Longri Ao, offered twenty-five rupees to anyone who could do the assignment.

Ro hesitated only for a brief moment. Twenty-five rupees would pay the cost of his trip home during vacation time. "I will do it," he offered.

He stripped to shorts, and, armed only with a small axe, a knife and fifty feet of rope, he tied one end of the rope to a post near the bridge and the other end around his waist.

If the current swept him away, at least the rope would give him a fighting chance. As he jumped into the water, his breath was snatched away by the frigid swirling current. When he surfaced, Ro prayed more urgently. So did the students, who were lined onshore on both sides of the raging river.

Ro let the river current sweep him into the middle of the jam. He started chopping and let the river take away the loosened branches. The heavy logs and tree trunks were another matter. He fought the tug of the current while trying to hack them loose from the jam. At times he felt he was chopping with a butter knife instead of an axe.

Four grueling hours later, Ro saw the final branches and tree trunks break loose and begin to drift downstream. He shouted triumphantly, and his voice was all but drowned out by the cheer that went up from the students watching on the riverbanks.

Ro let the current carry him to shore, and he pulled himself out of the river, tired but exuberant. The Bible teacher reached out his hand to pull him up. "I knew you could do it!" he shouted. "You have earned your vacation!"

During that summer vacation, Ro took a rickshaw to the train station and rode two days on the train. He transferred to a bus at Silchar and finally reached Lakhipur on the Barak River.

From there he planned to travel upriver by boat for his trip home. It was still a time of excessive flooding, but Ro convinced a reluctant boatman to ferry him upstream for a price of two rupees a day.

The Bengali boatman tried to talk him out of it. "Look up there, at the mountains where it is raining—we will have more flooding in two days, when the waters come down from the mountains. We must wait five days, until after the waters pass and the river drops," he told Ro. "If we leave now and have to stop until the flooding goes down, I'll have to charge you for the time we wait."

He pointed to his small boat, narrow and flimsy—with only enough room for one person to sleep under its small thatched canopy. But Ro was anxious to get home. "That is all right," he said. "We must leave now. I will pay two rupees for any day that we have to stop."

Ro packed four days' worth of provisions (just in case), and they started out. The boatman's prediction proved correct. Swollen rainwater pushed the river above flood stage just two days into their journey. They had to stop. But the rains kept on.

They tied the small boat to a tree that was already ten feet under water and waited. But every few hours they had to retie the rope higher on the tree branches as the waters continued to rise. Still the floodwaters did not recede.

The next morning they awoke, and the water was still at its highest level. Ro and the boatman spent another night sleeping in the tiny boat. There was no place for them to go for shelter.

Finally, Ro's provisions were gone. They had no food. "As soon as the river subsides," Ro told the boatman, "I will go to a village and buy some rice."

"But the next village is quite far. We must go back," the Bengali replied. "We have no food."

"My God will supply our needs," Ro told him. "He has promised me so." But they didn't even have water to drink—the river was so muddy.

But at last the rains stopped. Ro prayed that God would provide them with food so they'd have the strength to battle the strong currents and complete their journey.

Then Ro looked across the swirling waters of the river. "I think it looks calmer on the other side," he said to the boatman. "We can leave now and make up some of the time by rowing upriver on the other side."

The boatman was dubious. "It is only an illusion. The waters are just as swift there," he said. But since Ro was convinced otherwise, they tried to get their boat across the river.

For a long time they struggled, with the current pulling them downriver nearly half a mile before they finally reached the other side.

But suddenly and without warning, the boat struck a huge boulder under the water that sent a wave washing over the bow of the boat, and they were swamped.

Both men frantically tried to keep the craft from capsizing altogether. The front of the boat was almost totally underwater, overflowing with muddy river water—and something else. Ro saw something flopping as they bailed the water from the boat. It was a *masheer,* a huge fish, nearly two feet long and weighing nearly twenty-five pounds!

At the edge of the riverbank, Ro grabbed at an overhanging branch and pulled. The boatman also managed to catch a branch, and they somehow got the boat beached. Ro grabbed the huge fish by the gills and lifted it high. "My God has provided us with food!" he shouted joyfully.

The boatman was thoroughly impressed and nodded vigorously. "You have a great God," he admitted.

The Bengali cleaned and cooked some of the fish over a small fire. They kept some for the next day's meals. The two men slept with full stomachs that night. The next morning they ate more of it for breakfast. There was still a big portion of fish left over. Ro wrapped it in a big leaf and carried the small treasure to a village nearby, where he bartered it for a chicken. Now their supplies were restored.

For two more days they rowed the boat up the Barak River, which was now becoming much calmer with the level of the water dropping. When the Bengali boatman finally poled the boat to shore at the end of their journey, he took Ro's luggage out of the boat and set it on the ground. After Ro paid him, he looked at Ro and said, "Your God must be big!" He said it at least three times with emphasis.

Ro responded, "My God is *very* big. He owns the whole world."

Tears came down his face as he reached over and hugged Ro who told the boatman, "Yes, my God is big. He knew I needed to go home and see my parents. He provided a job so I could earn my way. When I needed protection, He watched over me and helped me. And when we needed food, he provided a huge *masheer*. Yes, my God has supplied all my needs."

In his final year at American Baptist Jorhat Christian High School, Ro used the two-week Puja holiday period in October to visit Nagaland. There he preached in village churches. Since that episode earlier with the Ao Naga students who had threatened him, Ro had developed a love for the Ao Naga people. They received him warmly into their churches and homes. It was not uncommon for him to visit a church and have six or more families vying to have him visit their homes for a big meal.

It got to be almost comical. Ro started a breakfast meal with one family, and another family would come, saying, "You have eaten enough here. Now you must come and eat at our home." And the same thing would happen at the next home. Typically he'd have to eat in the homes of many families and accept their hospitality.

In his last year of high school, Ro learned that he had successfully passed the university examination, which qualified him for further education. He left the mission high school at Jorhat, but his love for the Ao Nagas would never fade.

# Chapter Five
## *Testings and Triumphs*

Ro was penniless after paying his final high school bills. How would he manage the fifty rupees a month of expenses that it would cost him to study at St. Paul's College? Putting it into perspective, Ro recalled that fifty rupees was twice his father's monthly salary.

"I have a little savings," his father offered, pulling some rumpled bills from a hiding place in their small bamboo house. Deeply touched, Ro counted out the bills. There were fifty rupees, only enough for the first month. But the gesture caused him to see the depth of his parents' sacrifice. With their entire meager savings, along with a loan from K. Luaia, a brother-in-law, his parents were sure Ro would make it with his great confidence and faith.

After traveling four difficult days on foot and another four by train, the Hmar youth arrived nearly exhausted in Calcutta, a place Kipling called "the city of dreadful night." For an education, Ro reasoned, he could put up with the stench, noise, dirt, and masses of pushy beggars.

Even before the train pulled to a stop at Calcutta's Sealdah station, eager porters were climbing through the compartment windows. One grabbed Ro's bedroll and walked off. "Wait!" Ro called. "Where are you going?"

When Ro caught up with him, the man snatched his suitcase as well and rushed to a nearby *tonga* (horse-drawn carriage). Ro's luggage was already piled onto the seat of the *tonga*.

Intimidated, Ro fished out a small coin and gave a tip to the porter, who frowned and went back to the train.

"Where are you going?" the tonga driver demanded.

"St. Paul's College—Amherst Street," Ro answered. He recalled that someone told him the trip was a short ten-minute drive from the train station, but the driver was taking a different route, one that went up and down narrow streets and away from the busy highway.

It was dark now, and the "ten minutes" was long past. Then, the *tonga* driver turned into a dark alley and stopped. He pulled a long dagger from his belt and grabbed Ro's arm.

"Give me all your money, or I'll push this dagger right through you!" he threatened.

Frightened for his life, Ro did as he was told. The man shoved him out of the *tonga* along with his suitcase and bedroll. As the man drove off, Ro picked up his belongings, piled them upon his head, and started out in the darkness to find Amherst Street.

After an hour of walking, looking for a landmark to find his way, he stumbled upon Amherst Street. Then he somehow determined the direction of St. Paul's College and headed in that direction.

It was after midnight when with great relief he finally arrived safely at St. Paul's College.

When Ro signed up for classes the next day, the registrar insisted that Ro write his last name on the form. "I am Rochunga, from the Leiri clan of the Hmars," he said proudly. "That was all I needed in high school."

"It is not enough here. We must have a surname for our records."

Ro thought a moment, then he wrote "Pudaite," meaning "descendants of Pudai."

Ro was unable to pay even the first month's fees because of the robbery of the night before. He was willing, even eager, to work. But in this terribly impoverished city of Calcutta, there were countless applicants for every available job.

Ro shared his predicament with Dr. Eddy, the principal, who was sympathetic to his plight. Dr. Eddy encouraged him by telling him about new scholarships that were available for tribal people. Immediately Ro filled out the form and applied for a scholarship.

However, his application was turned down because the Hmars were not on the national census list.

So at Dr. Eddy's suggestion, Ro wrote directly to Prime Minister Jawaharlal Nehru in New Delhi. "I am a tribal, born in tribal territory of tribal parents," he stated. "I cannot understand why I do not qualify for a scholarship."

Shortly afterward the first installment for six months' tuition was granted.

The weekly Youth for Christ rallies in Calcutta helped keep Ro's focus on his long-range goals. The twenty-four-year-old student was a regular participant in these rallies, the largest in Asia, which attracted up to a thousand people at each event.

In Calcutta Ro met and entertained Frank Benson, a visiting official from the mission that had deposed Watkin Roberts. Ro felt it best not to discuss anything regarding Mr. Young Man with Benson.

Through this contact, Ro was hired by the mission during his college vacation. He was to travel to Manipur, visit and inspect the mission's schools, confer with the teachers during the day, and speak in churches at night. It was a busy time, and Ro became well known to the tribal leaders, not just as Chawnga's son, but as Rochunga of the Leiri clan, Rochunga Pudaite.

\*     \*     \*

In his second year at St. Paul's College, Ro studied English literature, ancient and modern history, economics, geography, and an extra English language course for further improvement. He knew he must pass the upcoming Intermediate of Arts (I.A.) exams in order to continue working toward his B.A. degree at a university.

After taking the exam in April, Ro returned to his Hmar homeland and waited confidently for the results to be announced in June. To earn money for his next year's education, Ro and a cousin teamed up to sell a ton of dried chilies.

After loading the chilies aboard a rented boat, Ro and his cousin Ringa began rowing down the rising Barak River toward Lakhipur.

As they approached their destination, the river was wild and at flood stage. As the tropical darkness began to envelop them, one of the top baskets of chilies caught on an overhanging bamboo and caused the boat to lurch and almost capsize in the roaring, swirling water.

The current pulled them into the middle of the flooded river. Straining every muscle, the two men fought to bring the boat to shore, when it suddenly lurched again and smashed into a larger boat. The prow of Ro's boat ran aground and stopped instantly with water swamping the back of the boat. Their small boat wobbled and bobbed in the current, then stabilized.

Exhausted, they tied up for the night. When dawn came, they inspected their cargo. Many of the chilies were soaked. When they finally got their damaged goods to market, they had to be content with half of their expected price.

While in town, Ro went to the telegraph office to pick up the results of his I.A. exam. There, he read in shocked disbelief, "Regret you are unsuccessful." Ro felt as if he'd been kicked in the stomach. "*Un*successful!?"

He was utterly broken. He had already applied to the famous Allahabad University for completion of his B.A. degree. He even had a government scholarship. How could it have happened? Now his entire future seemed to be in doubt.

Finally a gentle voice spoke to his heart. *I love you, Ro. You must first suffer the cross before you can enjoy the crown. Go back to Calcutta. You have more to learn of me before you go on.*

Reluctantly, Ro went back and sat down with his parents to discuss his future. Both Chawnga and Daii agreed that he should return to Calcutta and repeat the I.A. course.

Then Ro gave them the bad news. "There will be no scholarship this time. I do not see how it is possible."

Daii looked at her son with great and tender determination. "I will plant a *jhum* this year so we will not have to buy rice. And I will grow

71

chilies, ginger, and turmeric to sell. We will send you all of your father's salary. My hands will hold the hoe and not put it down until you receive your degree."

Ro was humbled by such sacrifices from his parents. He *had* to go back to Calcutta.

Returning to St. Paul's in 1951 was like rubbing salt in a wound. His eyes downcast, Ro tried to avoid other students as he walked across the campus. He felt even worse when he learned that he had failed only one subject—*by one point*—and ironically, the course was the extra English class that wasn't even required. However, the Indian system called for the student to get a passing mark in every subject—if he failed one subject, he failed the entire course.

Ro had passed the required subjects, failing the extra one that was not required, so he reasoned he should still be able to get his scholarship. He took his case to the scholarship committee, but they didn't renew his scholarship.

He wrote again to the prime minister, explaining the situation. Then he shut himself in his room for two weeks, praying constantly.

Ro was then attending Carey Baptist Church (named in memory of the great missionary Bible translator, William Carey). After spending another day praying for his scholarship, Ro went to church and heard a visiting American speaker from Youth for Christ, who impressed him greatly.

Bob Pierce told of his experiences of preaching in China before that vast nation had fallen under the dictatorial control of the communists. Pierce, now working in South Korea, told of refugees, war orphans, and the terrible suffering of the Korean people. Yet in the midst of their suffering, the Korean Christians did what they could to help others. Pierce spoke to the sixty or seventy people in the Carey church as if they were the only people in the world who could help the suffering Koreans.

When the offering was collected, Ro placed all of his money in the offering plate. He had to do something for the suffering and hunger of people who had never heard the name of Jesus. After the program, Ro met with Pierce briefly; then the visitor had to leave for another engagement. But the American's contagious concern for suffering masses in Asia had infected Ro.

While he was still praying about his scholarship a few days later, a postman came to the door and gave Ro a package. It was addressed to him but had no return address. Inside the package was a leather-bound English reference Bible. The inscription in the Bible read, "From a friend in America who loves the Lord and the people of India."

Ro read it from Genesis to Revelation. Then he did it again. And again. As a result, his English improved, and he found new power with the language. The Book also brought great spiritual understanding as well as inspiration to do the translation of the Bible into Hmar.

Then, a few days after this, a letter came from New Delhi informing Ro that his scholarship had been renewed.

What a relief to know his mother would not have to work so hard! Now Ro was certain that the Lord truly did have some special things in store for him during this makeup year in Calcutta.

On Saturday a letter came with funds for six months' tuition, room, and board. Ro counted the money and made plans to pay the registrar on Monday. On Sunday a lady from the Bible society, Mrs. Bowker, spoke at Carey Baptist Church. She described the need for printing the Bible in the Tibetan language. Mrs. Bowker said that the translation had been completed just after the war, and now they needed money to print the Bibles for the people of Tibet.

When she finished, the pastor, Walter Corlett, came forward to take the offering. Ro began to fidget. He wanted to help, but all he had was the money sent for his scholarship.

"You've heard the story of the Tibetan people," the pastor said. "You've heard that the Bible is translated into their language and is ready to be printed. There is no other book that will help them as much as this Book. We are going to take an offering. Give generously so that Mrs. Bowker will not have to go to other churches begging for the Tibetan Bible."

Ro looked at the floor. His heart was telling him to use the scholarship money he had in his pocket. *Give everything,* his heart told him.

His head argued more logically. *No. Give ten rupees. You can earn money to replace it. But not if you give it all. Besides, ten rupees is a large gift. You have never given ten rupees as a single contribution before.*

The pastor continued, "We are going to take the offering now." Ro was still struggling with the battle of his heart and his head as he prayed.

The offering plate went by without Ro seeing it. He was secretly relieved and told himself that he would pray for Mrs. Bowker.

The pastor got up again. "I am going to do something that I've never done before. I'm going to put the offering basket in the back of the church, by the door. If you haven't given all you can, here's another chance."

During the remainder of the service, the war between Ro's heart and head continued. But his heart won. On the way out of the service, Ro dropped in all of the scholarship money. Now without bus fare, he had to walk the five miles back to his dorm, but he did so with a singing heart that told him, *God will reward your faith. This is a lesson that you will never forget.*

It was true. The experience was one of many that would teach him to live by faith.

Back at school, Ro felt the twin realities of joy and fear, knowing he had acted in absolute faith by giving all to God in trust that He would be able to pay his tuition and other school expenses.

He would trust God. The first miracle took place two days later. After the early morning prayer meeting, Ro came to the gate of the college. There the gatekeeper gave him an envelope. He took it and looked at it.

It was an ordinary white envelope with *Rochunga* written on it in pencil. Ro looked at it curiously. There was no return address. He opened it. Inside was a one-hundred-rupee note. There was no letter or any explanation inside as to who had sent it to him, or why. Ro put the money back in the envelope and praised God for his timely provision.

And every time his tuition bill was due, God miraculously provided for every expense. It was a lesson well learned.

All things considered, the extra year *was* very profitable—perhaps not financially—but in acquiring the qualities of commitment, dedication, trust, obedience, and spiritual maturity. When the I.A. exam was given again, Ro did very well. Now he'd be going on to the University of Allahabad.

*     *     *

Allahabad, in the northern state of Uttar Pradesh, was quite different from the city of Calcutta. It was hot but not humid and stifling. The city was large and heavily populated, but it was not congested like Calcutta. Everyone here spoke Hindi, not Bengali, as they did in Calcutta.

At his Allahabad University dorm, Ro was treated royally. Servants swept the floor, made his bed, filled his drinking water jar, polished his shoes, and even spread his mosquito net at night. It was a strange new world to the young tribesman from Manipur.

Yet, of the five thousand students at Allahabad University, there were only twenty-two Christians. They formed a Student Christian Movement (SCM), which Ro attended. At the first meeting, he suggested that they make evangelism the focus of their activities.

His proposal was quickly rejected; the others wanted the group to provide social life and fellowship. Ro was warned, "If you are a fanatic who insults others by preaching about your faith, you will walk a lonely road here!"

In fact, his "lonely road" began the next day when he went from door-to-door in his dorm handing out gospel tracts. Some students took them politely, but others ripped them up in front of him, yelling obscenities. The students seemed convinced that Rochunga was part of "the white man's conspiracy."

Changing tactics, Ro invited students to come to his room and hear of his experience with Christ. Many came to listen, debate, or enter into animated discussions.

Ro's next real test of faith came in the classroom, where he learned that his Hindu and Muslim professors were knowledgeable and knew their arguments better than he knew his Bible. A teacher in comparative religions said Christianity was a "topsy-turvy religion where God seeks after man. The truth is," he declared, "man seeks after God. God need not seek, if he is God. That's where Christianity is wrong."

Confused, Ro went to the library. But the more philosophers he read, the more logical the professor's arguments appeared. Spinoza, Hume, Descartes, and Voltaire, as well as India's most prominent Hindu and Muslim philosophers, left him completely bewildered.

Alone in his room, Ro studied the Bible, only to discover that his teacher was right. The Judeo-Christian God was the "seeker." From Genesis to Revelation it was so. The words of the professor echoed in his ears: *God need not seek if he is God.*

Haunted by the problem, Ro sat in his classes like a mute statue. His intellectual knowledge of God had been tried and found to be lacking.

Sometime later Ro lost a prized pen upon which he had carved his initial, *R.* He knew he would recognize it if he could find it. He searched for the pen, off and on, for at least a week. Then, he stumbled upon it one day under a hedge, where he had recovered a shuttlecock during a badminton game. There on the ground was his pen, the one on which he'd carved the *R*.

The thought came to him, *Why have I been spending so much time seeking this pen?* The answer was suddenly obvious. *It is my pen. I bought it. I even carved my initial on it. The pen was unable to seek me. I had to seek it.*

The connection with his philosophical quandary was also obvious. *Of course, God is the seeker! He created man in his own image and put his "signature" on us, but man disobeyed God and became lost. And just as I searched for the lost pen that was mine, God seeks those he has created, those who are lost.*

His theological uncertainties evaporated like a mountain mist in sunlight. More mature and assured, he returned to the hill country just after his junior year. During his short vacation he taught in a private school and earned fifty rupees a month. As an incoming university senior, he was already one of the best-educated members of that private school faculty.

That fall, 1953, Ro discovered that the Congress Party's working committee was meeting at the Allahabad residence of the prime minister. Ro had long wanted to meet Nehru personally and thank him for the scholarship and tell him about the Hmar tribe. He feared that if government recognition was not offered to his tribe, some of the Hmars might become involved in the growing revolutionary activities. Already there were those who wanted the northeast area to break away from India and form a separate nation.

Ro tried phoning for an interview, but as he waited for his call to be put through, a no-

nonsense voice said, "Sorry, you must hang up. We have too many important calls."

Not to be deterred, Ro donned his best suit and tie, walked quickly over to the prime minister's residence, and asked the guard at the gate how he might get in for an interview. "Impossible," was all the guard said.

He tried a different tack. Removing his Western style suit and tie, he wrapped himself in the traditional Hmar tribal *puon* (a long striped shawl), and wiggled his toes into sandals. He strode purposefully back to Nehru's residence where, thankfully, there was a different guard on duty.

"I am Rochunga Pudaite," he grandly announced, "from the hills of Manipur to see the prime minister!"

The guard looked at Ro with a measure of confusion. "I am sorry, sir, but you will need a permit," the guard replied politely.

Ro was about to ask how to get such a permit when the guard pointed to a man who was approaching the gate. He said to Ro, "That is Mr. Lal Bahadur Shastri, a member of the cabinet. He can tell you how."

Ro introduced himself to Mr. Shastri and announced his mission. "Mr. Nehru is taking a short rest just now," he told Ro. "But perhaps you would like to see his daughter, Indira Gandhi."

Ro eagerly agreed and was ushered to a porch, where she was sitting. He was introduced, and she invited him to sit and have tea while giving his report.

The charming young lady listened intently as Rochunga told about his large tribe that was not included in the official census papers. She seemed surprised when he pointed out that in the four thousand square miles of Hmar lands in Manipur and Assam, there was not a single post office.

Nearly forty-five minutes later she asked, "Do you have this information in writing?"

Ro assured her that he did and pulled out several typewritten pages from a folder he had carried with him.

"You must see my father," she said as they stood, and she led him to the living quarters, where Nehru was just coming out of his room. Indira stopped her father and introduced Ro. Nehru listened to a brief summary of what the tribesman had shared with his daughter, then took the typewritten pages that Ro had compiled.

"I will certainly read this," Nehru told Ro. "I may call on you if I have questions. Will you be coming to New Delhi?"

"I will come if I am needed," Ro replied.

On his way back to the university campus, Ro felt an incredible sense of destiny. A real relationship had been established. He thanked God for the opportunity that he had been given and prayed that the prime minister would act on his proposal.

# Chapter Six
## *Flirting with Politics*

During Ro's senior year at the university, his studies and preparation for the translation work on the Hmar Bible were his most important goals. He had begun translating in his spare time, concentrating on the Gospels.

However, he still made time for Youth for Christ work and had been helping with the publicity for an upcoming YFC rally featuring Bob Pierce. One day while Ro was with Pierce, the American suggested, "How about going with me to Calcutta for a three-day rally?"

Ro was pleased to revisit the city but most delighted for the chance of getting to know Pierce better. The American was still helping YFC but was in the midst of forming a Christian welfare agency called World Vision, recruiting American sponsors for Korean War orphans. During that weekend, Ro spent time with the tall American and shared his longing to finish the translation of the Hmar Bible and to help with the development needs of his tribespeople.

Bob Pierce listened intently, then asked, "How would you like to go abroad for further education? I think that will really help with your translation work."

"I would love to," Ro answered, "but can such a thing be possible?"

"Well, you put in your application for a passport. It'll take some time. Meanwhile, I'll see if World Vision can sponsor you."

Ro filed for the passport right away, hoping that it might be issued by the time of his graduation in the spring of 1954.

Early that year, he received a letter from the prime minister's private secretary inviting Ro to New Delhi. He made the arrangements and traveled to the nation's capital with his roommate, Chiten Jamir (who later became finance minister of Nagaland).

Prime Minister Nehru had been meeting with U.S. ambassador Chester Bowles, who was just leaving.

In his meeting with India's leader, Ro presented Prime Minister Nehru with more information on tribal needs. Nehru then arranged for Ro to meet with the man in charge of such matters, Dr. Kaka Kallelkar, a member of parliament and chairman of the newly formed Schedule Caste and Schedule Tribes Commission, who assured him that the next census and list of tribes would indeed include the Hmars.

Then he asked Ro, "Are there any other tribes that have been overlooked?"

Ro nodded, "Yes, sir, I have a list of them." And he gave Dr. Kallelkar a list of many others that would not have easily been recognized without Ro's pointing them out. The list included the Paite, Zo, Gangte, Simte, Vaiphei, and others.

"Thank you, sir," Ro said gratefully. "Now young people from the tribes of northeast India will be eligible for scholarships."

While he was in New Delhi, Ro learned that all the important people in the Indian government always read the English-language newspapers. Articles about the Hmars in these publications would create an awareness of his people and the tribal needs. Back in Allahabad, Ro had hardly unpacked before he started writing articles.

As his senior year advanced and his graduation approached, Ro wrote and studied for his final exams, polished some articles, and translated more Scripture. "God has done so many wonderful things for me this year," he wrote to his parents. "I do not know what he really wants me to be. Please pray that I will not miss his best."

His first article, "Hmars—the Little Known Tribe of Northeast India," published in the English daily paper, drew a lot of response, including one from the prime minister and Dr. Verrier Elwin, Advisor to the Government of India for Tribal Affairs, a department newly established by Prime Minister Nehru.

Ro still had not heard from the passport office. But as he waited, more and more of his articles were accepted and printed in the Allahabad and national newspapers. Nehru had read them and invited him back, this time to stay at Constitution House, the official national guest residence.

Shortly after his graduation, Ro once again visited the capital. When he entered the prime minister's office, Nehru smiled broadly and asked, "What can I do for you now?"

"Sir," replied Ro, getting right to the point, "suppose you had a son away in school, and every time you wanted to write to him, you had to walk eighty miles. How would you feel?"

"That would be a hard proposition," Nehru replied with an enigmatic smile.

"Sir, since I was a high school student, my father has walked over six thousand miles just to send me letters. I will be going abroad for further study, and I would very much like a post office near my home so my father will not have to walk so far."

The prime minister was clearly impressed and asked Ro other questions about the tribal lands, the people, the languages, and their needs. Ro sensed that the powerful leader of India's millions was genuinely trying to identify with all of his people. As Ro was leaving, Nehru said, "Leave an address where you may be reached. I will certainly look into the postal matter."

A train trip took Ro back to Manipur. While he was in an Imphal hotel, chatting with a few tribal friends, a uniformed government messenger served him with an official-looking document. Ro looked at the paper at once. It requested his immediate attendance at a conference with the postal engineer and inspector of post offices.

Taking his friends along, Ro hurried over and was received with great respect. The official who met him bowed graciously and said, "Sir, Prime Minister Nehru's secretariat has instructed us to consult with you about opening four post offices in the hills for the Hmars. Can you suggest some locations and postmasters?"

While his friends looked on in amazement, Ro picked out sites for the first four post offices in his tribal lands and gave four names of tribesmen to be postmasters. These four post offices were opened by the end of that same year.

From Manipur, Ro traveled to Shillong to meet with Dr. Verrier Elwin. Prime Minister Nehru had introduced Ro to Dr. Elwin, who was a former British missionary who had come to India and was overwhelmed by the people and the culture.

He abandoned his religion and had gone back to the university in England to study anthropology. He had even rejected his British citizenship and become an Indian citizen and was serving as a civil servant. Dr. Elwin made his headquarters in Shillong, the capital of northeast India.

Prime Minister Nehru had suggested to Dr. Elwin that Ro be appointed as an officer in the civil administration of India. On Saturday Ro came to Shillong and checked into the Ferndale Hotel before going to meet with Dr. Elwin at his residence to discuss the prime minister's idea.

Dr. Elwin was a tall man with broad shoulders. He had let his hair grow long in the Indian style, although many Indians were now favoring the short, Western-style haircut. He puffed noisily on a pipe, and the room soon filled with its smoke.

"Well, Rochunga," he said at last, "I've read some of your newspaper articles. I must say, I'm quite impressed with your mind and practical wisdom.

"I'd like you to work with me as a research officer. To begin with, you'll have a rank of assistant political officer," he said smiling.

Ro grinned appreciatively. "That sounds wonderful."

"Excellent," said Dr. Elwin. "Now, I'm afraid I have some other business to attend to. How would it be if we met tomorrow and discussed the details over dinner?"

"Tomorrow?" Ro asked. Tomorrow was Sunday, and he was preaching at a Mizo church service in the morning. "What time tomorrow?"

Dr. Elwin told him to come at noon, and Ro knew that he'd have enough time to preach at the

Sunday worship service at the Mizo church and get to Dr. Elwin's residence in plenty of time. So he agreed to meet him then.

The next day after the service Ro didn't have time to go by his hotel room, freshen up, and leave his Bible. Instead, he hurried directly to Dr. Elwin's home right after the service.

Dr. Elwin opened the door for Ro and ushered him inside. Then Dr. Elwin saw the big, black leather-covered Bible that Ro carried and suddenly his eyes narrowed.

"I see that some ill-informed, ignorant, short-sighted missionaries have ruined you!" he snarled.

Ro was caught off guard. "Dr. Elwin, I do not understand."

"Don't play games with me! You know what I mean. I'm talking about that big book in your hands that you insist on showing off."

"B-but, Dr. Elw—"

The tall man interrupted Ro. "You will not work with me if you are going to carry that book. It will do no good to you or anyone else! Let me tell you—I came to India as a missionary. I was so religious that they called me Father Elwin. But I soon learned that dry theology was no good for anyone."

Ro blinked and opened his mouth to speak, but the man continued his tirade.

"I gave up Christianity and went back to Cambridge to study something worthwhile. I repeat, with that Bible in your hand you will not work for me. White missionaries have ruined you!"

Finally Ro was able to speak. "Dr. Elwin," he said softly, "I did not meet any white missionaries until my high school days. I became a Christian through my father. Almost our entire tribe now believes in Jesus.

"I didn't mean to offend you by bringing my Bible, but I had no time to stop by my hotel room after church services. Yet you must know this. Without my Bible, I cannot live. So I tender my resignation."

Just then the meal was brought. The two men sat at opposite ends of the table, and neither spoke during the entire meal. At the conclusion of the meal, Ro rose politely and thanked Dr. Elwin.

"Wait," Dr. Elwin said. "Do I understand correctly that you have an appointment with the governor later this evening?"

"Yes," Ro replied.

Dr. Elwin rose abruptly and grabbed the telephone. "Get me the governor!" he barked into the mouthpiece. After a brief wait, he was connected. "Your Excellency," he said with words as smooth as butter, "I'm calling about the young man who is coming to see you. Yes, that's the one. Well, I must tell you that this man is worthless. I have dismissed him and suggest that you do the same!"

Ro went back to his hotel with bitter tears flowing down his cheeks. The prime minister had wanted him for a "dream" position, and now it was being yanked from his grasp. He was hurt, angry, and confused.

In light of what had happened, he was not even sure he should go ahead with his appointment with the governor, but he remembered a promise he had made to a young science student, Laltuoklien Sinate, to appeal for a scholarship in a medical college for him.

On his way to the governor's compound, Ro wondered if the governor of Assam would be as rude and unceremonious as Dr. Elwin had been.

Mustering up as much self-esteem as he could, Ro went to the gate of the governor's mansion and tentatively gave his name to the guard at the gate.

"Yes, the governor is expecting you. You may enter." The big iron gate swung open, and Ro was escorted toward the mansion by Krishna Murty, the governor's private secretary.

Governor Jairamdas Doulatram had been standing in the doorway and walked toward Ro with arms outstretched. He greeted him with a big hug. Smiling he said, "What did you say that Dr. Elwin did not like?"

"I did not say anything, sir. He was angry because I was carrying my Bible. I was in the room when he told you that he dismissed me, but that is not true. I resigned when he told me I could not carry my Bible and work with him."

"Yes," the governor laughed, "Dr. Elwin can be quite arrogant sometimes. But come inside. I want to talk with you. You see, I count more on the word of the prime minister than that of Dr. Elwin."

The governor called for his private secretary to take notes of the meeting. Servants brought tea and cookies.

"Now," said the governor, "I want the full story of your meeting with Dr. Elwin so I can report back to the prime minister. How did you become a Christian? Who converted you?"

Ro was glad to give his side of the story. "I became a Christian before I ever saw a white missionary, sir. It was through the preaching of my own father." Ro's honest answers triggered more questions from his listener. Governor Doulatram was sincerely attentive and seemed genuinely interested.

Finally he asked Ro, "Why is it so important for you to be a Christian and carry your Bible?"

"Your Excellency," Ro replied, "if I do not have enough conviction to stand up for my faith in my God, then I do not think I could ever be a good citizen of India.

"I must have conviction and know where I am going. My faith in God and my Bible give me this guidance," he said.

Suddenly Governor Doulatram rose and went to Ro. He hugged him affectionately. "My son, India *needs* young men like you. We should not be discouraging them. Consider me like your father while you are here in Assam. If you need anything at all, come to me. I will be happy to arrange a number of scholarships for Hmar young people."

Soundly reassured, Ro left for his home. Upon reaching Phulpui, he found that the exciting news of his reception by the prime minister's office and the governor, as well as news of the plans for the new post offices, had preceded him. Ro had become something of a celebrity. Chawnga and Daii beamed when they heard the news, but they brought things back into focus by taking time to pray and praise God, thanking the Lord for all the opportunities that he had given to Ro, but expressed their gratefulness to God that some opportunities had been lost and would not distract him from his true goals.

Ro's achievements quickly spread across his Hmar homeland, and one day a delegation came to ask that he help organize a Hmar political party. "We have no hospitals, roads, or schools of our own. You met with the prime minister and won post offices for us. You can help us with these other needs."

The group stayed two days, pressuring him until finally Ro consented to serve as organizing chairman of the new party.

Ro was excited and a little awed by the responsibility thrust upon him. He discussed the situation with Chawnga. "Think of it, father. They might even elect me as the leader of the new party. What do you think of your son going into politics?"

His father thought for a moment before replying. "Perhaps it will be all right to help get the party established. But I feel that God has greater plans for you than just being a politician. While you go to the convention, your mother and I will remain here and pray for you."

The organizing convention was held in July in the centrally located village of Parbung, known for its frank-speaking, politically savvy people. News of what was taking place in Parbung quickly spread to every tribal village.

Ro wrote to Prime Minister Nehru, Indira Gandhi, Governor Doulatram, and many others, informing them of what was taking place. By runners he sent messages to key tribal leaders in every clan. He hoped for full participation and representation from all of the Hmar tribe.

News of the upcoming political convention ultimately reached the Mizo Union, a party that wanted all the non-Naga tribals in Manipur and

Assam to be united under the name "Mizo." So their agents in Manipur did all they could to frustrate Ro's plans. But they were unsuccessful, and on the appointed day some two hundred Hmar delegates from the various clans met in Parbung.

The first order of business was to find a name for the new political party. Ro announced, "I would like to suggest 'Hmar National Congress' for our new party.

"The word *congress* will keep us in touch with the leading political party in India, and the use of *Hmar* will help bring our tribe into national prominence."

Everyone agreed unanimously. Next, they hammered out a platform that would give Hmars an effective role in local politics. They decided that since they were identifying with India and not the underground separatists, they could ask for representation in national affairs. Plans were made to find ways of increasing the income for the tribal people, of building roads and schools, and providing other help.

The first day of business concluded and everyone was exhilarated by a great sense of accomplishment. Tomorrow they'd elect a leader for the party.

As Ro walked back to the home where he was staying that night, he couldn't help but wonder, *What if they choose me? If they elect me, then I will be known not just in my own tribe but all across India. I might even go on to become a member of Parliament!*

The next day four nominating groups met behind closed doors to pick candidates for the office of party president. When they returned, they asked Ro to excuse himself during the nomination and election process.

*That must mean that I am one of those nominated,* Ro thought. But he was sorry that he was the first candidate asked to leave the room; now he wouldn't see who his competitors were.

He chastised himself for not having feelings of humility at the honor of being nominated and expressed his regret in prayers to God. "Lord, forgive my conceit. But you know how many plans I have for my people and how much I want to help them. Please help me to seek your will."

He heard loud applause coming from the convention room and knew the people had made their choice. As he stepped back into the room, the vice-moderator called him to the platform and told him quietly, "Rochunga, you have been elected unanimously. We will give you a few moments to collect your thoughts before you address the convention. Incidentally, there were no other nominees even presented."

*No other nominees? Unanimously elected? What an honor!* he thought as he sat down, then reminded himself, *What a responsibility! Lord, make me worthy of their confidence.*

When he stood to address them, the entire audience came to its feet as one, to honor the new president. All chatter stopped, and they paid him homage with absolute silence and respect.

Ro swallowed hard so his voice would not quiver and told them, "I accept the great responsibility that you have given to me to lead the tribe for the next four years. I thank you for your confidence in me."

He was losing the battle with his emotions and tried to control his voice. "My-my acceptance speech will have to wait. I will prepare something and address you tomorrow night."

As the delegates left, the news spread. Soon signals were being flashed from one village to the next until the entire Hmar tribal nation had the message: "The Hmars have a new leader, Rochunga, son of Chawnga."

The next day he entered the assembly and was greeted with a standing ovation. He felt like a king or prime minister. The heady business of the day appeared routine and everything seemed to be building toward the evening meeting, where Ro was to address the entire assembly.

As they adjourned for the evening meal, a runner came in, bringing Ro several important envelopes. One was a letter from Indira Gandhi, offering her congratulations for the new party. Another was from Governor Doulatram of Assam, sending his good wishes.

There was also a letter from the University of Allahabad, reporting that Ro had successfully passed his university exams.

At the bottom of the pile was a copy of an overseas cable sent from Toronto, Canada. It was from Watkin Roberts! Mr. Young Man was sending him a cable all the way from North America in care of a man in Lakhipur, who had thought the communiqué was of such importance that he sent runners with instructions to go night and day to get it to Rochunga. It had taken three days to reach him. Ro unfolded the paper and read it: "Inform Rochunga Pudaite my friends and I will pay for intensive Bible training in Glasgow or Scotland. Stop. Cable decision."

Ro was stunned. He had no idea that Mr. Young Man even knew that he existed. Since he hadn't heard anything about his passport application, he had assumed that it was not the Lord's will that he study abroad. Now, on the verge of accepting the political leadership of his people, a different, unknown door had opened.

He stood for a moment staring at the cable, rereading it several times. Finally, he was called to the dinner. His host sensed something wrong. "Mr. New President, what is it? Come. Eat and be happy. You are destined to lead us into greatness and fame."

Yet Ro was troubled by the decision that faced him. He went to the dinner and read them the telegrams from Indira Gandhi and Governor Doulatram. But again he asked to postpone his acceptance speech.

Rising the next morning while darkness still lingered, Ro heard a rooster crow as he walked across a deserted farm field.

He tried to deal with his dilemma using logic. Was it not God's leading that had brought him to this particular place of accomplishment and potential power? Here was a way to serve his people and his country. Here was a way to make significant strides.

As Ro reflected, it seemed obvious that the Lord had gone before him and opened all the doors in order for him to be at this place at this strategic moment.

*Yet, what about the cable from Watkin Roberts? Why did it come now? Is it that God wants me to consider this plan before I get involved with politics?*

For an hour he stayed there, weighing the two options. Then he prayed, pouring out all his feelings to God.

"My Father in heaven," he cried, "if you hear me, tell me what to do. If I reject the presidency, the new party that I brought into being may die. My people may lose hope. Yet, if I take this office and remain here, I may never be able to finish the Bible translation. Please tell me what to do. I am willing to follow either path."

In a moment the words *Glasgow, Glasgow, Glasgow* began ringing in his heart. At first he was puzzled, confused about his own analysis of what he thought to be God's leading. Was it taking the leadership of the tribe? It was most logical to follow that path.

Or what about the cable from Roberts?

Ro resumed his attitude of prayer. *What is it, Lord?*

The word echoed in his mind, then repeated itself incessantly. *Glasgow. Glasgow. Glasgow.* Fully assured that this was a direct answer to his prayer, Ro returned to face the expected displeasure of his people.

He returned to find his friends still sleeping. He washed his face, drank a cup of tea, then prepared for a new speech to deliver before the installation ceremony that evening. Sadly, Ro couldn't help feeling that he was turning his back on his people and a wonderful opportunity for unusual power and fame. But he felt compelled to obey God. Could he make them understand?

If anyone noticed how subdued and serious he was that day, no one mentioned it. When he came to the platform that evening, tribal leaders came forward with a *puondum* (tribal shawl). In the past this distinguished honor was given to an accomplished headhunter or one who could hunt and kill the most ferocious wild animals. Now, the robe was bestowed on tribesmen who brought honor to the tribe by other accomplishments.

The leaders draped the red, white, and black striped *puondum* upon Ro's shoulders. "You have brought honor to all Hmars," said the spokesman. "And we have confidence that as you lead us, our tribe will find greatness."

Ro was absolutely overwhelmed. Next they presented him with the feathered headdress given in past times only to great Hmar chiefs. The long *vakul* feathers of the "king bird" were placed on his head.

His thoughts were a confused jumble of uncertainty. *Lord, how can I turn my back on this mandate from my people? Are you certain that you want me to do this?*

Once again the words rang in his ears: *Glasgow. Glasgow. Glasgow.*

He stepped to the podium and looked into the faces smiling up at him, expectantly. "Lord, help me," he breathed, and he began to speak-- telling them what had happened.

He concluded, "So I therefore tender my resignation. I want all of us here to pray that God will lead us to another man to take my place. I will do all I can to help."

For a moment the audience sat in stunned silence. Then, as the shock wore off, there was a growing rustle in the crowd as the reaction of disbelief spread through the delegates. A few took Ro's comments at face value and knew he'd want to do the godly thing. Others, though, were not so charitable. They said, "He is leaving us for a better opportunity."

The choice was made to elect Lungawi, Ro's cousin, to replace him. Lungawi was a college student who spoke good English, and Ro felt he had the potential for doing a notable job for the new party.

Yet, Ro's spirit was uneasy. He had so many plans but had little confidence now that they could be carried out without his leadership.

"I'll pray for you," he told Lungawi. "If there is any way I can help, I will do so." The convention closed on this note of optimism.

Ro knew that his first need was for a passport. A Mizo Union leader in Manipur told him that this was impossible. Some people had waited many years to gain a passport and lately even well-connected people were being denied a passport completely. Ro had already been denied a passport when Bob Pierce asked him to apply. He had never even heard back from the passport office at that time. It was with this cloud of doubt hanging over his head that Ro went to Imphal to apply for a passport.

Knowing the absolute necessity of the document, Ro went directly to his scheduled appointment with Mr. T. Kipgen, the state passport officer in Imphal. But despite his best efforts, Ro wasn't able to get there as quickly as he'd planned. Mr. Kipgen was just locking up for the day when Ro got there.

"Sir, I have come to apply for a passport," Ro explained. "Can you help me?"

"Sorry," the man answered. "Come back tomorrow at ten o'clock."

Reluctantly, Ro went to a nearby hotel and rented a room for the night. He arose the next morning eager to complete his task. Although it was only a ten-minute walk to the passport office,

Ro decided to get there in plenty of time, so he left his hotel room a half hour early.

But before going downstairs he stopped at the rest room on the second floor.

Just as he was about to leave, he noticed a strange-looking burlap bag sitting by the sink. He bent down to look at it. There were crumpled newspapers on top of whatever was inside.

Ro reached into the bag, below the crumpled newspaper. His hand found a hard rectangular shape, then another. He pulled one of the small bundles out of the burlap bag. His eyes widened in amazement. It was a banded bundle of one-hundred-rupee notes, and each bundle had at least one hundred notes in it! He tried to put the amount in context. He recalled that his father earned twenty-five rupees a month as a pastor and evangelist.

Yet he was holding a fortune of ten thousand rupees in his hand! His father would have to work more than thirty-three years to earn that kind of money. This single bundle of rupees represented a life's savings.

Reaching back inside the bag, he found *still more* of the bundles. There must have been thirty or forty such packets. His quick estimation was that inside the burlap bag were at least *half a million rupees!* It was a staggering sum.

He'd never seen such a fortune before in his life. Ro's heart was racing, and his breath was rapid. Hurriedly he put the money into the bag and rushed back across the hall to his room. Once inside, he locked the door and laid out all the money on his bed.

He immediately knelt by his bed and prayed, "Lord, should I keep this money? Or do you want me to try and find its owner?"

Ro got no immediate answer, so he rose, put the money into his suitcase, locked it and put the case under his bed, putting the key into his pocket. Then, after remembering his appointment at the passport office, he locked the door of his room and started down the stairs.

Coming up the stairs from downstairs was a distraught man, half sobbing, half groaning. "I'm dead!" he cried. "I'm a dead man! O-oh, I am dead!" Ro heard him cry out to his Hindu deity. Then he watched as he went into his room across from Ro's and shut the door. His wailing could be heard even from behind the closed door.

Tentatively Ro went to the man's door and knocked. "Go away!" the man inside called out.

Ro knocked again, this time insistently. The man finally opened the door. "Go away," he repeated. But before he could shut the door, Ro pushed against it.

"Sir, can I help you?" he asked.

"No. No one can help me! I am a dead man," he groaned. The man pushed Ro out of the way and shut the door again.

Ro went to his own room and tried to think of what he should do. *Surely this is the person who is the owner of the money,* he thought. *And I have tried to help him. Since he is already convinced that it is gone, maybe the Lord intends for me to keep this money that I have found.*

Ro wrestled with that idea. But he had not tried very hard to tell the man he could truly help him. Ro hadn't told him that he had found the money that the man had misplaced. His claim to the money was growing weaker.

Ro decided to try again to help the man. He went back to his room and knocked at his door, but when the man opened the door and saw it was Ro, he didn't even speak. He simply pushed him away and shut the door again.

Shaking his head, Ro went back to his room again. *That's it! I have tried to talk to him, but he rebukes and refuses me. It must mean that I am to keep the money. He lost it, and I found it. I can do much good with it.*

But no sooner had his mind framed the words of that idea that he was rebuked. It was almost as if the Lord's words were audible. *No! The money is not yours. You cannot keep it. You must give it back.*

Ro knew this was the right thing to do. A third time he went back to the man's room. This time he forced himself inside. "Please," the man wailed, "I cannot talk to anyone. I am dead. My gods have failed me."

"But I can help you," Ro told him.

"No one can help me," the man cried.

Ro took the man's arm and pulled him toward the hall. "Come with me," Ro said simply. "I want you to see something."

Stubbornly the man pulled back, but Ro's tug was insistent and stronger. He pulled the man into his room.

Once inside, Ro reached under the bed and grabbed his suitcase. He took the small key from his pocket and unlocked it. Then, with a grand sweep, he opened it and dumped the full contents onto his bed. The bundles of money seemed to take up the whole bed.

The man's eyes widened in amazement, just as Ro's had done earlier.

"My money! *My money!*" the man cried out in exultation. He looked into Ro's smiling face and nodding acknowledgment. "Yes," Ro said, "it is your money."

The man fell prostrate at Ro's feet in the Hindu gesture of utmost adoration. After Ro's embarrassed efforts to get him back on his feet, the man quickly regained his confidence.

"But you could have kept my money, and you have given it back. Why?" he asked.

Ro told him, "My God reminded me that it was not my money, that it would be wrong to keep it, even though I had found it. My God told me to find its true owner and return it."

"Your God is special!"

The man began putting the money back into the burlap bag. He introduced himself and explained how it all had happened.

"My name is Agarwal. I came from my home in Calcutta, sent here by my father, to start several petrol stations in Imphal. And as there are no banks, my father sent me here with all cash. These rupees are to acquire the land and to start construction of those petrol stations.

"I left this morning for my meeting with the land owners to buy the property for the stations. But when I got to my meeting, I discovered to my horror that I did not have my money! Instantly I recalled having stopped in the rest room as I was leaving and knew I must have left the bag of money there.

"And when I got back and checked, it was gone. I felt it was gone forever. I believed that no one finding it would return it. Anyone who found it would surely feel it was a gift from the gods."

"But it was your money, Mr. Agarwal. Much as I would have liked to keep it, my God told me that I must return it."

"I will reward you for your honesty," said Mr. Agarwal. He reached over and took several of the bundles of rupee notes and handed them to Ro. He had an armload of thirty thousand to fifty thouand rupees which he held out to Ro.

Ro shook his head, waving the money away. "This is your money," he said emphatically. "I cannot take it."

"No, I insist," Mr. Agarwal said.

Again Ro declined, pushing the money away from him.

"Please, I want you to have it."

"No. Thank you, Mr. Agarwal, but I have already wrestled with the problem—should I take the money?—and my God told me that it was not mine. So I cannot take it—*any* of it."

Mr. Agarwal looked stunned. Then he said quietly, "Your God is *very* special indeed. And so are you."

When the two men had shaken hands and bid each other best wishes, Ro started for the passport office. It was nearly ten o'clock so he hurried downstairs, and hailed a rickshaw to take him down the street to his destination.

He got to his appointment on time, and Mr. Kipgen asked Ro why he needed a passport.

"I plan to study in Europe," he replied.

"Really? Where in Europe?"

"Glasgow, Scotland."

"Well, in order for me to issue you a passport, you will need at least two persons to vouch for you," Kipgen explained.

"That will not be a problem. I have many friends who will gladly do that."

"Let me finish," Kipgen said. "These two character references must be people who have over ten thousand rupees in hand or own land worth one hundred thousand rupees. Or, a first class officer in the government service also qualifies."

Ro was crestfallen. "I don't know anyone like that," he said sadly. "Who can I go to?"

Then he thought of the man he'd just rescued from financial ruin. "Have you heard of Mr. Agarwal from Calcutta?" Ro asked the passport officer. "He certainly qualifies."

"Yes, I know him. He is quite wealthy. But he is from Calcutta. Your references must be local people."

"But I don't know any local people who have that kind of wealth. Could *you* do it, Mr. Kipgen?" Ro asked.

The passport officer laughed and shook his head. "I am the passport-issuing officer. I cannot do that."

"Then can you give me the names of any who can be references for me?"

The man thought for a moment, then wrote the names of two people on a piece of paper. Ro took the paper and smiled. "And if it would not be asking too much, could you kindly give me a letter of introduction in order for me to meet them?"

Surprisingly, Mr. Kipgen agreed to Ro's request. Ro went to see the two men, the first a wealthy businessman named Mr. Daiho and the second, a high civil servant. And remarkably, both men agreed to be character references for Ro.

Back at the passport office, Ro turned in the letters vouching for his character. Mr. Kipgen shook his head in disbelief. "Your God must really want you to go to Glasgow!" he said, smiling. "Stop back in three days, and your passport will be ready!"

Ro marveled at how God had paved the way for him. In less than one week, he'd miraculously received approval of his precious passport!

When the passport was received it was truly something of an occasion. Only a handful of Hmars had ever traveled outside the country. When they did, it was generally as soldiers in the Indian army. None that Ro knew of had ever gone as civilians. Ro held the small passport and fingered its pages lovingly. Truly this was a miracle. And it was another proof that Ro's decision was the right one.

The day after the passport arrived, Ro went home to say good-bye to his family. After the farewells, his father and two close friends accompanied Ro on the long trek to Silchar and waited as he boarded his bus to take him to the airport. From the window Ro snapped their picture with his new Agfa camera.

Ro flew to Calcutta and preached in the church that he had attended as a student. Afterward the members gave him a farewell party and Pastor Walter Corlett pronounced, "On behalf of Carey Baptist Church, I commission you, Rochunga Pudaite, as our Indian missionary to the West!"

After the farewell party, Ro was alone in his room at the Corletts. Tomorrow he would leave for Scotland. He tried to visualize what lay ahead.

Humanly speaking, it was difficult for him to get over his resignation from tribal leadership. Here he was, at the height of his popularity and power. He could have asked for almost anything, and his people, even government leaders, would have responded.

Now, all he had was uncertainty. Soon he'd be on his way, across oceans and continents, to a land where nobody knew him, where he had no recognition, power, or even friendships.

All Ro had to cling to was his faith in his heavenly Father and the assurance that it was God's will.

# Chapter Seven
## *Glasgow!*

On August 24, 1954, Ro boarded a KLM Super Constellation that was to take him to Europe. It was his first time away from his beloved homeland.

"Will you be having a cocktail before dinner, sir? Then how about a soft drink?"

"Would you like a pillow or blanket?"

"Sir, would you like to read a magazine?" The glamorous Dutch cabin attendants on the KLM flight to London made Ro feel like royalty. All his life he had associated white faces with power and authority. Now, three beautiful young women, dressed as fashion models, were waiting on him— a strangely delightful but pleasant new experience.

Too excited for sleep, he took out his Bible and read from Isaiah 43:1-3:

> Fear not: for I have redeemed thee, *I have called thee by thy name; thou art mine.* When thou passest through the waters, I will be with thee; and through the rivers, they shall not overflow thee: when thou walkest through the fire, thou shalt not be burned; neither shall the flame kindle upon thee. For I am the Lord thy God. *(emphasis added)*

What reassurance! Surely if the Lord had called him by name, certainly he would give him guidance and provision. Ro sat back in his seat, looking forward to the future.

The plane took him to Karachi, Tehran, Beirut, Istanbul, Frankfurt, Amsterdam, finally landing at London's Heathrow Airport. Ro spent two days in London, then traveled by train to Scotland. As the train sped northward across the countryside, Ro was fascinated by this strange new land.

In London he had seen milk bottles delivered right to the doorsteps. He wondered if only wealthy people could afford such a luxury. Newspapers were stacked in piles at corner newsstands, where people could pick one up and toss a coin in a cup; it seemed that commerce was on the honor system.

As the train continued rushing along the countryside, Ro saw the well-planted fields with tractors pulling huge pieces of farm equipment in seamless, straight furrows. The train passed industrial cities with factories. On the nearby roads he saw cars and trucks in abundance but saw no ox-drawn wagons, *tongas*, or rickshaws anywhere.

When he reached Glasgow, he stood for a while outside the train depot and gazed at everything. The sidewalks were bustling with hundreds of factory workers and other crowds, but there wasn't the congestion of Indian cities.

Glasgow was an old city with grimy, soot-blackened stone buildings. The streets were packed with people and crowded with more automobiles than Ro had ever seen at one time before.

He soon learned that he had to be as wary of speeding cars as he had been of tigers in the jungle. Both could do deadly harm if they came upon him.

The Glasgow Bible Training Institute had fewer than a hundred students, in contrast to the five thousand or more at Allahabad University. Only one other student besides Ro was a college or university graduate. Some of his Scottish classmates hadn't even finished high school.

Fortunately, Principal Andrew McBeth was quick to understand the problem and took a keen interest in Ro. "Mr. Pudaite," he said in his thick Scottish brogue, "you have made significant progress in your studies in India. You are ahead of most of the students here. I'm afraid that the classes may not be difficult enough for you. But I have an idea. Tell me, how would it be if I arranged for you to study Greek and Hebrew at Glasgow University?"

"It is as if you have read my thoughts," replied Ro, grinning widely.

The months went by quickly, and Ro found himself experiencing his first really cold winter. In his homeland the temperatures were always mild in winter. Only in the mountains did they see frost or freezing.

But the extreme cold, coupled with the dampness of Scotland, made him shiver. He did not own an overcoat, nor could he afford to buy one. So the cold rains and icy winds from the North Atlantic were difficult.

One day was really remarkable, however. Ro awoke one morning to see the entire outdoors absolutely transformed. A clean blanket of white had covered everything during the night. In the morning the sun had come out, and the entire landscape glistened.

"Oh, that's just snow, a bit early this year," he was told casually.

Ro had never seen such a sight. He had seen snow before, but it was on the top of faraway mountains. Here it could be handled.

He ran outside into the yard to touch it, hold it, throw it into the air, run in it. He knocked it from the tree branches. Naively he took a bucketful into the house to save it, only to watch it melt.

His studies at the Bible institute were structured to prepare him for practical Christian service—teaching, preaching, and evangelizing—rather than the work of Bible translation. However, at Glasgow University he was able to study the classical biblical languages. Ro's hard-earned mastery of English while in school in India now gave him a means to conjugate verbs and understand the tenses of Hebrew and Greek.

Just as he had learned English by using the English *Book of Common Prayers* and the Bible, Ro used Hebrew and Greek Bible texts to help him understand those languages.

Meanwhile Ro continued to work on his Hmar Bible translation. Chapter by chapter, the manuscript began to grow thicker. Ro made frequent trips to London to consult with Dr. William Bradnock, translation secretary of the British and Foreign Bible Society, which had agreed to publish the Hmar Bible.

Dr. Bradnock was encouraging and helpful, and Ro was even invited as a guest to his country home in Kent.

But he was also grateful for the emphasis of the Institute on practical service. All his life he had made it a practice to preach and witness to others.

By spring Ro had begun to get invitations to speak at Scottish churches and evangelistic rallies. Often an honorarium of ten shillings (about $1.35) was given, but that generally went for bus fare, lunch, and other expenses related to the speaking engagement. Nevertheless, these experiences gave Ro a chance to practice English as well as to develop his preaching style.

On occasion he would go out with other students as an evangelism team from the institute for street-corner witnessing and door-to-door evangelism. By this time his Indian-made shoes had worn out. The snow and rainy weather had split the soles, and his shoes were falling apart.

Ro tied them together as best he could, but it soon became obvious that he had to buy a new pair. He wasn't certain that he had enough money, but decided to go shopping for a new pair anyway.

It turned out that it wasn't a money issue. He went to many different shoe stores in Glasgow, but the salesmen all said the same thing: "Sorry. We don't make size five in a man's shoe."

He came back to his room discouraged. The shoes were beyond hope now. Ro did have a pair of canvas sneakers that he'd bought in India, and now, had to wear them in the middle of this Scottish winter.

He kept trying. Shoe clerks told him to try the boy's department, and he tried that, but men's feet do not fit well into boys' shoes. Finally, in despair and frustration, Ro went to Dr. McBeth, the principal, and told him his problem. He remembered hearing of the many times Dr.

McBeth had shared with the students how God had answered his prayers when he was a missionary in Africa.

"Do you think God can help me find shoes?" Ro asked him.

"Sure he can," Dr. McBeth replied. "Let's pray right now."

After the two had prayed, Dr. McBeth said, "I know exactly where they will have the kind of shoes you need."

He took Ro to a store where Ro had been earlier in the week. "Sir, I have already been to this store, and they do not have my size," he told Dr. McBeth.

"Then I know of another store."

When they got to the next one, the clerk recognized Ro. "He's already been here," he told Dr. McBeth. They went to another store. It was the same story.

Then Dr. McBeth brightened. "I know! I'll take you to the boys' department. . . ."

But seeing Ro's expression, he knew that this idea had already been tried as well. Dr. McBeth drove Ro back to his room, and Ro walked around Scotland another week in his flimsy sneakers.

A week later he found himself strangely drawn back to Burton's Men's Shop on Queen's Street. It was one of the biggest shoe stores in Glasgow. But he'd already been here twice before with no success. At first he resisted the impulse to go in, but something inside pulled at him.

This time a new salesman greeted him. "May I help you?"

"I would like to buy a new pair of shoes," Ro replied.

"All right. What size?"

"Five."

"Hmm—let me go check." He was gone a few minutes and came back shaking his head. "We don't carry that size anymore."

Just then the man who had waited on Ro the other two times came up, recognizing him. "You don't give up, do you?" he said with a smile. "I wish we had shoes in your size, but we don't. Sorry."

"But surely you have them," Ro argued, now feeling that this was why he had been drawn into the store.

"Perhaps we should, but we don't."

"But you *must* have them," Ro said.

The manager came out. "What's he talking about?" The salesmen explained the situation.

"Sir," Ro said to him, "I think you have my shoes here. I came to get them."

The manager looked at his feet. "What size do you wear?" When Ro told him, he said, "Can you wait here for just a moment?"

Then he turned to the salesmen. "You remember that Spanish fellow who had small feet? We had some handmade shoes crafted for him, and I don't think he picked up the last pair. They were here a long time. I wonder if he ever came in for them."

The manager walked to the back of the store and soon returned with a shoebox. He opened it, and inside were two shoes that looked as though they might fit.

Ro sat in the chair and tried them on. They fit as though they had been crafted for his feet. "What is the price?" he asked.

"About £100," the manager said. Ro felt the air rush out of his lungs. (At the exchange rate then, it would put the price at about US $271.)

Ro looked at the shoes on his feet. He had never had any shoes that fit so well or looked so good. "They are wonderful, but—"

The manager sensed Ro's discomfort. "Lad, how much money do you have?" he asked the young man.

Ro pulled all the money he had from his pocket. It was twelve pounds. The manager took the money, smoothed the wrinkled bills, and counted them along with the handful of coins. Then he said, "Take the shoes home with you."

Ro couldn't wait to get back to Dr. McBeth's residence and when he answered the door, Ro just stood on the steps, grinning. Then Dr. McBeth looked down at his feet.

"Ohh-h," he said admiringly, "You must come in so that we can properly thank God."

\*     \*     \*

"I am so amazed to find so many in Scotland who need our Savior," Ro wrote to his father in India. "There are drunkards, prostitutes, thieves, and beggars, just as in Calcutta. I am shocked. I suppose I was expecting it to be more like heaven here, in a country from which so many missionaries have come."

One day at the turn of the year, the Glasgow Christians were preparing for an upcoming 1955 crusade by the famous American evangelist Billy Graham.

Professor D. P. Thompson, director of evangelism for the Church of Scotland, invited Ro to travel with him as part of the "Tell Scotland Campaign," the group that had invited Graham to their country.

Basically, Ro's part was to go door-to-door and distribute information about the crusades and witness to the people he met. During these weekend trips, Ro had the joy of helping several people come to know his Lord.

One day while Ro was having lunch at the Bible Institute, a man ran breathlessly into the dining hall looking for him. "Ro!" he called across the room. "It's Billy Graham calling for you!"

Ro dashed to the telephone. Actually the caller was Dr. Paul Maddox, Billy Graham's personal assistant, on the other end of the line. "Mr. Graham has heard of you and your efforts and would like to meet you. Can you come to see him here at the Northern British Hotel?" he asked Ro.

"I will be there in five minutes!" Ro told him excitedly. He had barely replaced the receiver when he realized that he may have been too hasty in saying he'd be there so quickly—the hotel was at least a mile away and he had no transportation.

Ro ran outside and looked in vain for a bus or taxi. None were in sight. Then, without hesitating, he began running as fast as he could in the direction of the Northern British Hotel.

He reached the hotel totally out of breath but in less than ten minutes. He met Dr. Maddox in the lobby and was still panting as he was led upstairs to the Grahams' hotel room. It was enough time for him to regain his composure. By the time he knocked on the door to the room, he had caught his breath.

Billy Graham and his wife, Ruth, were sitting on the bed. He was introduced to them and to George Beverly Shea and Cliff Barrows, who were sitting on a nearby steamer trunk. They all greeted Ro. Then the evangelist waved him over to a small sofa to sit.

At first Ro was awestruck by the tall American evangelist and the others. He recalled having the same sense of wonder and shyness when he had first met India's prime minister Nehru some years earlier.

However, Graham's casual manner and down-to-earth humility soon eased any sense of initial intimidation. Billy Graham's interest in the young man from Manipur was genuine, friendly, and sincere.

"I've heard reports from various prayer groups that your whole tribe back in India is praying for our crusade in Scotland," he said.

"It is true," Ro replied. "My father has organized all-night prayer meetings and a chain of prayer from one village to another."

"And is it true that your father walked over a hundred miles to read a Bible after he was converted?"

Ro was amazed at just how much was known about him and his people. "Yes," he answered. "Missionaries were not allowed in Hmar territory, so my father had to walk all the way to a neighboring state in order for him to get Bible training. Then he returned to evangelize our own people."

"A remarkable story," the team agreed as they all began asking Ro questions about this indigenous work in India. Finally, he told them about his work in translating the Bible.

"That's amazing," Graham said; then, after looking at his watch, he stood up. "I'm sorry. I'd really like to stay and talk with you some more, but I have a luncheon appointment. You'll forgive me if I excuse myself."

Ro also stood and shook hands with the evangelist. "Where are you studying?" he asked Ro.

"At the Bible Training Institute here in Glasgow," Ro answered.

"Are you satisfied with your training?"

Ro replied with simple honesty, "No. I believe that I have learned all I can at the institute. It is time to move on. I have an offer of a full scholarship to Oxford University in England. But I am not sure if that is where God wants me to be."

Graham asked, "Why don't you come to America? It might be a better place for you to do your translation work."

Ro could only blink in response.

The evangelist said, "I'll make all the necessary arrangements if you want to come to Wheaton College Graduate School."

Still surprised, Ro did not know what to say. "Th-thank you. I—uh—I will pray about it. Thank you so much for your kindness."

As he left the hotel, Ro was already running the idea through his mind. It did not take him long to decide to accept the offer. He remembered that Bob Pierce, founder of World Vision, had already offered to sponsor him, and had implied that he should come to America to study. In fact, Wheaton was the school that Ro had in mind when he had first considered Pierce's offer, but when he hadn't heard from the Indian passport office, he had given up the idea and gone to Allahabad.

Now perhaps the timing was right, and God wanted him to do this. Ro sent a message to Bob Pierce to ask his counsel. He promptly replied:

> "Yes, Ro. I do remember that when you were in India I offered you a scholarship to come to America. My offer is still good. I would like you to let Billy Graham arrange your entrance and admission to Wheaton College, and World Vision will take care of the finances. I will have my office send you money for transportation to America."

While correspondence moved back and forth to the U.S. concerning his admission to Wheaton College, Ro continued to work on the first draft of the Hmar New Testament. With a strong sense of accomplishment he showed his manuscript to Dr. Bradnock, who very patiently described the sequential steps of revision and correction that would have to be done prior to its publication.

In the spring of 1955 Ro got the good news of his acceptance by Wheaton College and applied for his U.S. visa. When the American consul in Glasgow insisted on seeing Ro's birth certificate, Ro told him that when he was born, no such documents were issued in the tribal areas. "But as you can see, I have indeed been born," Ro persuaded him. Finally, after considerable pressure, Ro convinced him to issue the visa.

Ro received a check for $153 from World Vision for passage across the Atlantic. It was the figure Ro had given Bob Pierce, being the cost for the cheapest berth on the ocean liner.

Unfortunately, that economy fare was also the choice of other students and tourists traveling in the summer. When Ro went to the travel office, he was told that no economy berths were available, nor would they be for the foreseeable future. Everything was booked.

"Please," Ro told the clerk, "kindly put me on your waiting list, and call me when you have a cancellation. I will pray that God will find a place for me."

That was in June. *Surely something will open during the next few weeks so I can travel across the ocean in time to register for fall classes in September,* Ro thought.

By mid-August no cancellations had come through. Ro began asking, *Did I make the right decision?* He almost regretted having turned down the full scholarship to Oxford University.

On the last Friday of August, Ro became anxious. He told his roommate, "I have set aside the entire day to pray about this problem. If I am to go to America, I must get a space on the ship by Monday. Will you pray with me?"

Late that afternoon, John Moore, the superintendent of Gospel Tent Hall, knocked on the door. Ro had often participated in gospel services there. The Gospel Tent Rally had been started by the famous nineteenth century evangelist Dwight L. Moody and continued as an outreach to the city of Glasgow. Each Saturday evening some three to four thousand people attended the rally.

"Ro, I need a favor," Moore asked him. "The speaker we had scheduled for tomorrow night has

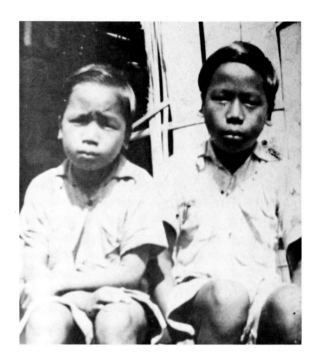

*Ro, age 7, with his older brother, Ramlien.*

*Ro in high school photo, left, and ten years later.*

*Ro and his new bride, Mawii, on their wedding day, January 1, 1959, just before they left for America.*

*Senvon Village.*

*Ro and Watkin Roberts, about 1960.*

*Ro and Mawii started village schools as a way to help their people. These were the first Hmar graduates of the Sielmat Christian High School (above) in 1962.*

*The school library (below) shown in 1971 photo.*

Since 1959 more than 300 churches have been started in northeast India. Ro's brother, Ramlien, dedicates this church in Binakhandi, (above).

Ro meets Indian president, V. V. Giri, (below).

*The beginnings
of Bibles
For The World*

*A test mailing of
New Testaments in
1972 launched*
Bibles For The World.

*Ro and Mawii mail
one-millionth New
Testament.*

*Russian Bibles
were printed and
sent from India as a
part of a cultural
exchange.
Some Christian
leaders are convinced
that sending Bibles to
Russia during the
Cold War might have
had a part in
concluding
it more quickly.*

# BEYOND THE NEXT MOUNTAIN

*The lives of Ro, Mawii, Chawnga (Ro's father), and Watkin Roberts are featured in this powerful, dramatic motion picture.*

Scenes from the movie (clockwise from top left)

1. "Mr. Young Man," Watkin Roberts.

2. Ro and Mawii.

3. Chawnga as boy (played by John Pudaite).

4. Chawnga receives the first Hmar Bible.

# The India Children's Choir

*Bibles For The World auditioned these boys and girls from northeast India to be part of the first India Children's Choir that came to tour the U.S. and Canada.*

*Mary Pudaite-Keating, Ro's daughter, (right) is shown with young Hmar girl. Mary was the executive director for the India Children's Choir and went to India in 1989 to recruit and train the five choir tour groups.*

suddenly canceled. Would you be kind enough to be my speaker?"

Ro was flattered by the request, but said, "No, John. I am sorry, but my English is not good enough to preach to so many. I cannot do it."

Six-foot-tall John Moore bent down to Ro's eye level. "Take it this way, Ro," he said, grinning. "You have no reputation to destroy. If you do well, it'll be a great beginning for you. If not, who's going to remember?"

"All right." Ro smiled. "But you must pray for me." Then he added, "Pray that I will get on the ship going to America."

The following evening Ro was nervous as he looked over the audience of several thousand people. He was still ill at ease when he began to preach, but as he started, God answered his prayers and gave him great confidence, ability, and effectiveness. When Ro gave an invitation, fifty-seven people walked forward to receive Jesus Christ as Savior.

After the meeting the hall emptied, and Ro returned to the platform to retrieve his notes and Bible. He was unaware that the microphone for the PA system was still on, so his remarks carried throughout the hall.

John Moore said, "Did you tell me that you were going to America?"

"Yes," Ro replied, somewhat subdued.

"When do you leave?"

"I-I do not know," Ro answered.

"What do you mean? You're going to America, but you don't know when? I don't understand," Moore said.

"Well, John," Ro explained, "I could not get a seat on the boat. But I need to be there, or I will miss the enrollment date for school."

John shouted from across the platform, "Ship. In Scotland when you say *boat* you mean that wee, little thing you go rowing in. What you mean is that you couldn't get a berth on the *ship*."

A moment later a well-dressed man strode up to the platform. "Excuse me," he said to Ro, "but the public address system picked up what you were saying. I heard you say you couldn't get a berth on the ship crossing the Atlantic. Is that right?"

"Yes," Ro replied glumly.

"Well, can I do anything for you?"

"No," Ro told him, "I do not think so. I put my name on the waiting list, and it has been nearly three months—"

"Maybe I can help," the man interrupted.

"You can pray for me," Ro said.

"I think I can do more than pray." The man smiled, and Ro heard him say, "My name is Alexander Stuart of the Donaldson Line, the largest ship line between Scotland and the New World. On each of our ships we reserve rooms for last-minute VIP travelers. I'll see that you have a room."

"But, sir," Ro interrupted, "I have only $153 for my ticket."

"It doesn't matter. Leave it to me." Mr. Stuart scrawled something on the back of one of his business cards. "Come to our office, and give this to the receptionist. She'll take care of it."

Ro was delightfully surprised, absolutely overwhelmed by this amazing turn of events. After thanking Mr. Stuart, Ro hurried back to his room to pack. It didn't take long for him to stuff his few belongings into a single small suitcase. That, in addition to his portable typewriter, would be his only baggage to the New World.

The next morning he went to the address that Mr. Stuart had given him. The receptionist there gave him an envelope and wished him a pleasant journey. He was on his way!

A steward met Ro at the dockside gangway. He took Ro's ticket envelope, looked at his special pass and saluted smartly. "Yes, *sir*, Mr. Pudaite. Welcome aboard! I'll get a porter to bring your baggage aboard right away."

The steward snapped his fingers in the direction of the porter. "Escort Mr. Pudaite to the VIP stateroom, and bring his baggage aboard," he ordered.

Ro meekly offered his small suitcase and typewriter case. The porter looked around for more. "Is a limousine coming along to bring your baggage, sir?"

"No, this is all I have," Ro answered quietly. The porter took them and led the way aboard and along the corridors to his room.

On the top deck they walked through a spacious corridor and stopped at a door marked VIP Stateroom #1. The porter unlocked it and waved Ro inside.

Ro had no idea what "VIP Stateroom" meant when Mr. Stuart had made the provision. He was not at all prepared for the magnificence of the quarters. They were beyond description. Ro was certain that they had made a mistake and would surely come soon to move him to the lower-class berth.

The porter showed him the facilities. "This is the entry hall, sir. You can receive your visitors here. You can take them here, to the library," he said, waving to the adjoining room. The library had a tall ceiling with a chandelier and wide walls completely lined with hundreds of books.

"The library also doubles as a dining room, I'm afraid. I hope it doesn't make you feel cramped," the porter apologized.

*On the contrary!* Ro thought. *Even a king could live here in luxury!* It was finer than any palace or mansion that Ro could have imagined.

"And this is your private bedroom suite, sir. You'll notice that it has a nice bath." The porter concluded the tour of the stateroom after turning on the appropriate lights. As he left he asked, "Is there anything else I can do for you, sir? Perhaps I can polish a pair of your shoes before dinner."

The only shoes that Ro owned were on his feet, but he slipped them off and handed them meekly to the porter with a shy thank you. The porter saluted sharply and left, leaving Ro standing in the middle of the huge stateroom.

It took Ro just a few minutes to unpack his small suitcase. A little while later, he heard a soft knock at the door. He opened it and was greeted by two tall men who stood there with a military bearing. The first man, in a dark pin-striped suit, was serious and looked important. The other man, a little older, was wearing a tailored uniform. He saluted as the first man bowed slightly.

The man in uniform spoke first.

"Your Excellency," he greeted Ro, and then introduced himself. "I am the Captain of the ship. I want you to know that we are here for your comfort and service. If there is anything at all you need, simply press that call button, and we'll be at your door."

Ro gulped and started to speak but realized he had nothing to say.

The man in the dark pin-striped suit introduced himself as the ship's purser. He smiled and said, "Your Excellency, if you wish to dine alone, simply ring for the steward. But should you wish to dine in the public dining room, it will be the captain's honor to have you as a guest at his table."

Ro, still at a loss for words, managed to say, "Th-thank you. That is most—uh—agreeable.

"Thank you, Your Excellency," the men said in unison, came to attention, saluted, and walked away.

Ro closed the door and shook his head. *Your Excellency,* he smiled to himself. *As if I were someone important.*

On his bed was the Bible he had just unpacked before their visit. He had laid it out for his daily devotions. He picked up the book and started to read where he had left off before. The words suddenly came alive and virtually jumped off the page at him:

> Behold, what manner of love the Father
> hath bestowed upon us, that we should be
> called the sons of God. (1 John 3:1)

Ro put the Bible down for a moment to savor the richness of the moment. "Thank you, Lord," he prayed. "I am a child of the King, so you have arranged for me to travel like royalty!" Then he laughed. "Well, since I am a child of God, I may as well enjoy it!"

# Chapter Eight
## *Meeting Mr. Young Man*

The week at sea went quickly but was a rich experience for Ro. He was able to work with complete concentration on his translation of the book of Ruth into Hmar. He also preached at the ship's Sunday worship service. Having come so recently from the Billy Graham 1955 Scotland Crusade, Ro remembered how the evangelist had always given his listeners an invitation. So Ro gave an invitation at the conclusion of his shipboard sermon, although it was uncustomary at such services. Nevertheless eleven people came forward to receive Christ.

But now the ship would soon be docking in Montreal, Canada. Ro had made arrangements to travel to Wheaton, Illinois, by way of Canada so he could meet someone. He had cabled Watkin Roberts of his visit.

After the ship docked in Montreal Harbor, Ro traveled to Toronto by train, eager to meet the famous Mr. Young Man, the one to whom his people owed so much.

*What will he look like,* Ro wondered. *Will he still remember our people? Will he even recall spending time in our village? It was so long ago, and he stayed for just five days. I wonder if he will remember. . . .*

At Montreal Ro boarded the train that would take him on the next lap of his journey.

As Ro listened to the *clickety-clack* of the

train wheels that were bringing him closer to Toronto, he thought again of *Pu Tlangval* (Mr. Young Man), who was to meet him at the station. He'd heard about this man all his life.

Ro had seen an old photograph of him when he was a boy and had even corresponded with him during the past year. But the thought of actually meeting him made his heart beat faster— in sync with the train's racing wheels.

Next to his own father, there was no man Ro held in higher esteem than this spiritual father of his tribe.

The closer he got to his destination, the more excited Ro became. Finally, the train conductor came down the aisle. "Toronto. Next stop is Toronto."

Even before the train jolted completely to a stop in the terminal, Ro had bounded down the steps of the passenger car onto the platform, looking through the crowd. The old photograph would have been useless—it had been many years since Mr. Young Man had been in India, and Ro surely would not recognize him now.

As his eyes looked over the small crowd of people waiting for the train, Ro noticed a white-haired, stoop-shouldered, elderly man with sparkling eyes. He was using a cane and was quickly limping toward him.

"*I dam a lawm maw!*" the man called to Ro in the beautiful, flowing Lushai dialect.

Ro smiled and grinned. "Yes, I am well, thank you."

"You really are well, aren't you! My, my! I can't believe it. Imagine Chawnga's son being in Toronto. Welcome, Rochunga, it's so good to have you here."

A broad smile spread across Ro's face as the two of them embraced. The man had such warmth and sincerity in his greeting that it seemed they had always been friends.

Watkin Roberts introduced his wife, Gladys, and daughter, Ruth, and they started toward his car. As they walked, Roberts said, "I still love the people of India, Rochunga. I've never stopped praying for them, and for your tribe especially. And now, think of it—you've come to America to complete your education. What an answer to prayer!"

*Pu Tlangval* was no longer a young man. Ro had imagined him to be a tall, imposing person with thick black hair and dark eyes. That was the way Chawnga had described him. In reality Roberts was well under six feet tall and had snowy white hair. The cane was needed because of polio that he'd contracted in the thirties.

Ro judged Roberts to be in his late sixties. As they drove along, he observed, "I have been praying that the Lord would let me see at least one of your people before I die."

"How did you first learn of my people?" Ro asked.

"Well, when I arrived in India, I discovered a book by someone with the same last name as mine, but no relation. The book was *My Forty-One Years in India* by General Lord Frederick Roberts. It was full of stories about Hmar headhunters and described in detail the account of the tea plantation massacre. I actually felt the hair on the back of my neck stand up as I sensed God calling me to minister to your people.

"I had been in Lushai territory for several months and helped translate the Gospel of John into Lushai. Then I sent copies of the Gospel of John to every Hmar chief in the hills via native *dak* (mail) runners.

"A few of the chiefs could read and write in the Lushai language. Kamkholun, the chief in Senvon, Chawnga's village, was the one who had asked the *dak* runner to translate or interpret the book into Hmar. But he didn't understand it. So I received word a few days later that Chief Kamkholun wanted someone to come and tell him the meaning of the Gospel of John."

"So that is when you set out across the mountains," said Ro. "My father and his friends heard you singing as you approached the village."

Roberts chuckled. "Exactly. It was more to keep up my courage. I'll never forget when that Hmar warrior threw a spear that landed within inches of me!"

"They probably didn't know who you were at first," Ro observed.

"That's right. But when I told them that I had come to tell them about the Book—the Gospel of John. Well, they didn't cut off my head. Instead, they welcomed me as a brother. Their hunger for the gospel was tremendous." Ro saw that the old man's eyes were growing misty.

"Yes . . . ," Ro said quietly. "It is exactly as my father has told me."

"Ah, Chawnga . . . ," Roberts said, his eyes recalling the experiences of some decades earlier. "Chawnga was a timid young man at first. I once brought him to Aijal, where he spent time in my home learning. He went back to the hills and became a torch, setting the hills aflame with the gospel. His boldness as a preacher is a gift from God."

"Yes," Ro agreed as they drove along.

"Your father, Chawnga, memorized the entire book of John, verse by verse, before going back to his tribe. Remarkable!" Roberts continued softly.

"Why did you ever leave us, sir?" Ro asked. "Why did you leave India—your work had just begun."

Roberts looked the other way but not before Ro noticed him flinch at the question. His eyes suddenly grew sad, and his face could not mask the sadness and hurt. Yet he answered Ro without any bitterness in his voice. "I suppose I 'bent' too many rules by living under the same roof as the tribals and doing things differently than some of the other missionaries.

"I didn't follow the ways others wanted me to. For example, I encouraged the tribals to preach the gospel to other tribals—just as I did with your father. It was a totally new philosophy of missions. Before, the pattern was to have Western missionaries preach the gospel to the tribals. But I saw that as an extension of the old colonialist way.

"When you train a tribal preacher to take the gospel to his own people, you don't have to overcome major language and cultural differences. Yet it was too new, too different. It got me into a terrible muddle with all the other missionaries."

Ro listened quietly and began to feel the pain in the old man's heart.

"Rochunga, I was *expelled* from Lushai hills," Roberts said in a voice not much more than a whisper. "And they took away my mission organization and left my family and me stranded in Calcutta." The old man sighed deeply as if reliving the pain.

"You could go back to India now," Ro suggested. "Our country has independence and religious freedom now. No one can stop you from teaching and training our people to preach the gospel."

Roberts chuckled. "The hills of Manipur demand strong legs, Rochunga. Since my battle with polio some years ago, well—my legs aren't what they used to be."

The old man looked into Ro's intense face. "Besides, Rochunga, God worked exactly as I knew he would. He called me to sow the seed. I entrusted the rest to the Holy Spirit. And I was not disappointed."

"Yes," Ro agreed. "Today there are over a hundred Hmar churches in the mountains."

"S-so *many?*"

"And your early converts are now our elders and leaders."

Tears again welled up in the old man's eyes, and he turned from Ro's gaze. Then he looked back at the young Hmar man beside him. "Please try to understand, Rochunga. When I—when I was expelled, I went back to my trade as a chemist.* But I've always wondered what happened on those mountains when I left forty years ago."

Now it was Ro who was blinking back the tears. "We have not forgotten you, *Pu Tlangval.* My father still prays for you every day on the mountain. And because of your faithfulness, my father is still on fire for the Lord. His firm faith has kept my feet on God's path."

* *a pharmacist*

For a few moments no one spoke. Then the old man's face shone as if inspired with a great truth.

The missionary's voice cracked with great emotion. "Rochunga, the Lord has given me this moment to answer all those years of doubts, persecution, questioning, and frustration. What an amazing Christ!" he exclaimed. "He never seeks for our approval, Rochunga, only our obedience and the faith to believe that he is at work—even when all is mystery."

He leaned toward Ro. "To put one's life in God's hands is not to be led astray. You see, the Lord allowed me to sow the seed. And you—you, Rochunga, are the firstfruits of the harvest."

"*Pu Tlangval,* how did you come to send me the cable?" Ro asked, explaining that its timing had been so providential.

"Well, as I've told you," the old man continued, "I've continued to pray for Chawnga, Taisena, and the others. I've prayed that God would make it possible for me, my friends, family, and some others to help some Hmar leader come to the West and be educated and trained. I believe the day of foreign missionaries in India is coming to a close. If the gospel work is to continue in India, it must be under national leadership.

"One morning after I'd finished praying, I heard over the radio that an Indian lady was to speak at the Toronto Youth for Christ rally. I invited her to my office. It was Winnie Bonar. She told me about you and how you turned down a high government position rather than give up your Bible or deny your God. Then I found that you're the son of Chawnga, my friend and fellow soldier.

"Well, I simply bowed right there in prayer and asked God for wisdom. I sensed him saying, 'This is the man. Send a cable now—send a cable now.' So I did! And here you are!"

"It was God who planned it all," Ro told him, explaining how the Lord had timed the events on the other side of the world as well.

After dinner at the Roberts home, the two talked many more hours until late into the night before they retired.

Over the next few days, before Ro had to leave to register at Wheaton College, they had many more things to share, and a wonderful bond developed between the two.

Three days later, when his train to Chicago was leaving, Ro was overwhelmed with a sense of deep gratitude for having had the opportunity to meet this dignified, determined old man who had meant so much to his tribe.

As he left Toronto, it was with a renewed confidence that—just as his father had assured him long before—God's love had preceded him unto this new horizon, this distant horizon on the opposite side of the world from where his journey had begun.

# Chapter Nine
## *No Time for Culture Shock*

Ro had taken the train from Chicago to downtown Wheaton and was directed to the Wheaton College campus about a mile away. He picked up his small suitcase and typewriter and started walking. It was September, 1955, and the weather was still warm and pleasant.

He came to the campus, found Blanchard Hall, walked in, and asked the receptionist for information. "I am Rochunga Pudaite, from Manipur, India, and I have come to enroll at Wheaton College."

The busy young woman looked up from her typewriter and told him simply, "Just go over to the gym."

Puzzled, Ro turned and went outside, thinking, *I wonder who "Jim" is. He must be very important if everyone knows him by only his first name.* He'd already learned in Scotland that Westerners often shortened their names—that some had nicknames—which were what he was told these contractions were.

He asked the first fellow he saw, "Excuse me, do you know Jim?"

The student shrugged. "Naw, I'm new here myself. I don't know anyone yet."

Ro asked several others. "I must see Jim. Do you know where he is?"

They all looked as confused as he was. Finally someone recognized his dilemma. "Jim? Oh—you mean *gym*—it's short for *gymnasium*.

That's where the registration is going on." The young man pointed out the building to him.

Ro set his suitcase and typewriter down near the door to Blanchard Hall rather than carry them around with him. After all, this was America and no one would steal anything.

As he stood in line at the gym to register for classes, Ro listened to students laughing and calling to their friends as the new semester got underway. As best as he could figure, there were only six people in the entire United States that he had ever met—all missionaries—except for Billy Graham and his associates, whom he'd met in Scotland.

His stomach growled as the line moved slowly toward the registration desk. He had not eaten all day. Finally he reached the registration desk and filled out the requisite forms. Then he asked about his room.

The woman at the desk informed him, "Oh, it's our policy that graduate students are not permitted to live in a school dorm. You'll have to find housing off campus, I'm afraid."

Ro stood in line at the queue for housing. When it was finally his turn, the girl at the table looked for his name on the list and gave him an address. "We found a room for you to rent on Seminary Avenue," she said. "Here are the directions for you."

He walked back to Blanchard Hall to retrieve his suitcase and typewriter and wasn't the least surprised to see them still sitting where he had left them.

It was quite a few blocks to the address Ro had been given. It was already midafternoon as he walked along a tree-lined residential street, looking for the address given him. When he found it and knocked on the door, a lady came out and reacted with a strange look when he identified himself.

"Uh, I-I'm sorry," she said. "I've decided not to rent the room. I can't show it to you."

That seemed strange to Ro. The girl at Wheaton College had called ahead to tell the lady that Ro was on his way, and everything seemed to be in order then.

He walked back and explained to the housing coordinator what had happened, and she gave him another address. But when Ro knocked at the door of the home, it was the same as before—a last-minute decision not to rent.

Many homes near the campus had signs in a window: Room for Rent. So, rather than return to the school, Ro thought he'd inquire for himself and find a place to live. But each time that Ro asked, a homeowner would look at him carefully and say, "Sorry, our room has already been rented," or "We've changed our minds and decided not to rent."

Ro wondered why they had not taken down the sign if that was so. It finally became clear to him that the people were somehow put off by this brown-skinned stranger at their door. Everywhere the answer was always the same—*No*.

Ro decided to go to the faculty person in charge of housing. Mr. Schoenherr was most sympathetic and offered to take him to a listed room himself. But then another faculty member introduced himself to Ro. "My name is Dr. Harrison, and I'm head of the college Missions Department. Are you from Burma?"

"No, sir. I am from India. Manipur." Dr. Harrison said, "I was a missionary to Burma. I know the area where you're from. It's not far from the Burmese border.

"Please, Rochunga," he continued, "let me take you to this address." They got into his car and drove a mile or so from campus.

Then, at 103 North President Street, they pulled up to the curb. Dr. Harrison went with him to the door. They were introduced to a large smiling, blonde woman. "I'm Laura Bartlett. My husband and I have had students rooming in our home for twenty-seven years. This is the first year he isn't with me to welcome the new students. He died just a few weeks ago."

Both Dr. Harrison and Ro extended their condolences. Mrs. Bartlett's face clouded only for a moment; then she welcomed Ro with a friendly greeting and showed him a cheerful room in her home. "Oh, this will be wonderful, Mrs. Bartlett," Ro said. "I'll take it."

"Is that all the luggage you have?" she asked Ro. He nodded. "But you'll freeze here this winter. It's a long walk to school, and at twenty below, you'll at least need earmuffs."

Ro smiled, although he didn't know what earmuffs were.

By now the evening shadows were growing long. Ro walked a few blocks to a corner grocery store to buy something to eat.

He wandered up and down the aisles looking at the strange labels. In his homeland foods would be displayed in the open, ready to be prepared and cooked. But here, everything seemed to be in a box or can. Finally he selected a can of peaches and a fruit drink, then returned to his lonely room for his first meal since arriving in the United States at Chicago's Union Station.

The next day Ro recalled Mrs. Bartlett's kindness and wondered how he might do something for her. He went downstairs and learned that she had gone shopping for groceries. In the basement, he found an old reel-type lawn mower. He'd seen one like that at the Allahabad Oriental Mission Station. He took it outside and tried it out. The grass had grown quite tall. Ro figured that Mr. Bartlett had been the one who cut the grass, and now that he was gone, there was no one to do it. So he went to work.

By the time Mrs. Bartlett came back, he was just finishing. She looked at the job and for a moment just stood there biting her lower lip.

Sometime later, Ro observed that the windows were dirty. That, too, had no doubt been Mr. Bartlett's job. Ro got a bucket of water and began washing windows.

When he had finished, Mrs. Bartlett came out on the porch with a platter of freshly baked blueberry muffins and a huge bowl of ice cream. It was her way of expressing her gratitude.

As Ro sat on the porch enjoying the treats, she said softly, "Ro, how can I thank you? You don't know how much it means to me to have someone do these things. With my husband gone—" She began to get tears in her eyes.

"Mrs. Bartlett," Ro said, "these treats are thanks enough. And to see you smile once again."

"Thank you," she said. "You know, it's strange, for twenty-seven years I've had students renting a room in my home. But no one has ever done something like this for me. No one has ever done anything without being asked. And even then, I had to pay them."

The following week, when the turning of the leaves on the stately oaks and elms began Wheaton's annual fashion show, Ro was fully immersed in his work. Besides his classwork, he worked three hours every evening in the college library. The rest of his time was spent working on the Hmar Bible translation.

For inspiration, Ro wrote a devotional book for Hmars titled *Mountain Spring*. With church services on Sunday, he had only Saturday for free time. In this available "free" time he did his laundry, shopped for food, and cleaned his tiny room.

"You're too much of a grind," Howard Wood, another roomer at Mrs. Bartlett's, told Ro one day.

"Grind?" Ro questioned. "What is that?"

"Uh, it's American slang. It means you're somebody who works too hard. All you do is work and study and translate and work some more. What you need is a break."

"Break?" Ro was having trouble with all this American slang.

"You need to get away from all this work for a while. What you need is a date. How about letting me fix you up with a girl to go out with this weekend?"

Ro gulped. Although he was twenty-eight years old, he'd never gone out socially with a young woman. "No, thank you, Howard. I wouldn't know how to act. An American would laugh at me—at my ignorance of how to act."

"Nonsense," Howard replied. "Tell you what, we'll make it a double date. I'll take my girl, and we'll find you a date. We'll go out together, and all you have to do is watch me. It's easy. I'll even give you some lessons. What d'you say, Ro?"

Reluctantly Ro agreed, so long as Howard agreed to show him how to act. On the eventful evening, Howard and his date drove up in front of Mrs. Bartlett's rooming house to pick up Ro. A few minutes later, they were in front of the house where Ro's date lived. Howard briefed him. "Her name is Janet. Now all you have to do is go up to the door, ring the bell, greet her, and then escort her back to the car. You open the car door and shut the door behind her, then go around and get in the other side."

That didn't sound terribly complicated. Ro walked up and rang the doorbell.

"Good evening, Rochunga," Janet said politely as she opened the door for him.

Ro bowed ceremoniously in the Asian manner and said, "Good evening." He looked up at the young woman. Howard hadn't told him that she was tall—*nearly six feet tall!*

"Well," Janet said pleasantly in a soft Tennessee drawl, "I see that you're right on the dot."

Bewildered, Ro looked at his feet and shuffled to the side a few steps. He didn't see any dot on the steps.

"Y'all ready to go?" Janet asked.

More bewilderment. *What is a "yawl"?* Ro wondered. In his confusion he forgot Howard's instructions about taking her elbow and escorting her down the steps to the car. He scurried along several steps behind her, trying to catch up. Her long-legged stride made it difficult for him. When he did catch up and tried to reach for her elbow, he realized that she was much too tall for him to guide her gracefully, so he walked on tiptoes all the way to the car.

Everything seemed to be going wrong. After she got into the backseat and Ro shut the door, his coat caught in the door, and he thought she was pulling on him. Then he noticed, and quickly opened the door, retrieved his coattail, and got into the backseat on the other side. His cheeks flushed red with embarrassment, although no one in the car laughed at what he felt was gross clumsiness.

Finally they got to the restaurant. He watched as Howard stood behind his date as she sat down, and he smoothly pushed her chair toward the table. Ro tried it too. But Janet was already seated, and the chair wouldn't budge. With a sense of rising panic and embarrassment, Ro bent down, and putting his knee to the back of the chair, he shoved mightily. It was like moving a heavy boulder!

They ordered a simple American meal of hamburgers, fries, and Cokes. After the dinner Howard asked what kind of ice cream each wanted. "This place is famous for its ice-cream desserts, so let's really splurge."

Ro didn't know what to order. *Is "splurge" an ice-cream dessert?* he wondered. Just to be sure, Ro asked the waitress for a menu. But it was full of strange names: Rocky Road, Black Forest Surprise, Black Cow, Marshmallow Delight, Baked Alaska.

Then Ro saw something on the menu that he recognized. "I'll take a vanilla ice-cream cone," he said. When the waitress came back with the dessert order, she handed Ro the cone. The others had ordered various sundaes, which she served on dainty dishes poised on doily-topped plates. Ro felt like a silly child licking his cone.

Most of the conversation was beyond him. He didn't know who or what they were talking about, and Janet's southern accent compounded the problem. After someone had made a particular point in the conversation, Janet turned to Ro and asked, "Mercy—what ch'all thank 'bout thet?" Ro was absolutely mystified.

To his great relief, Howard dropped him off first and then took the girls home.

It took several days for the trauma of the culture shock to wear off. By then Ro had resolved never to date again, unless it was absolutely necessary.

He was certain that the Lord could find him a life partner without the complications and embarrassment of dating.

Fortunately, Ro's finances were better than his social life. His school fees were being paid by World Vision, and his student library job covered incidental expenses. So when he received word that an Indian medical student he had helped get a scholarship was having trouble making ends meet, Ro immediately began sending the student a regular portion of his small salary.

The cold Illinois winter blew in with an icy blast, and it seemed much colder than in Scotland the previous winter. The Wheaton temperature plummeted. Although Ro had survived the winter in Scotland without a topcoat, he realized he'd never make it without one in Illinois. Trips to and from the campus got colder and colder.

One day as he shivered in a classroom, another student told him that clothing could be bought cheaply at a rummage sale being held at a local Catholic church.

Ro wasn't sure what *rummage* meant, but he went along with the other student. Looking through a pile of topcoats on a table, he struck up a conversation with a friendly nun. He told her of his experience with Christ, and she said that she had met Christ only a few months earlier herself. He beamed in delight as the sister related her own conversion experience.

As they talked, Ro told her, "Americans are so big that I am afraid I will not be able to find a coat that will fit me."

The nun nodded. "There are some smaller sizes over there." She escorted him to a table piled with coats. Immediately a grey coat from the pile caught his eye. He picked it up and found that it was a beautiful tweed coat.

When Ro tried it on, it seem tailored for his narrow shoulders and small stature. But the coat must have sold for two hundred dollars or more originally, and the present price tag reflected its great quality. It was priced at twenty-five dollars, a huge amount for the shivering student.

"Is there some arrangement that I could make to get this coat?" Ro asked the nun. "I need it very much, but I cannot afford the full price just now."

"How much money do you have?" she asked him.

Ro emptied his pockets and showed her that he had just $1.50, a ludicrous fraction of the tagged price.

The nun went over to her superior. "We send clothes overseas to people in need," she told her. "Now, here is someone in need who has come to us. Can we help him?"

The older nun agreed, and they both came back over to Ro.

"Take the coat," the first nun said, smiling. "God loves you, and we love you, too. We will pray that your time in America will be profitable."

Ro floated home feeling indeed like a "child of the King." It was also a great feeling to walk in the cold air protected by this wonderful warm coat.

One morning early in December not much later, Mrs. Bartlett asked her foreign boarder to come home right after his last class. "Don't go to the library. Don't eat at the Student Union. Just come right home," she insisted.

Not knowing what she wanted but having become so close to the kindhearted widow, whom he regarded as his American mother, Ro wanted to please her. So he promised he'd be there.

That evening he walked into the house and saw all of his friends from church and school waiting for him. "Surprise! Surprise!" the friends shouted. And began singing "Happy Birthday."

Nobody had ever sung "Happy Birthday" to the young Asian before. Touched by their love and friendship he couldn't stop the tears from spilling over. There was a beautiful cake, and everyone brought a card. After they had eaten the cake, he began opening the cards and was even more touched by the gifts of currency tucked inside each one.

After they had eaten the cake, he finished reading all the cards and counted $127 in gifts. It was enough to meet his personal expenses for the entire winter!

Ro's heart overflowed with gratitude at their love. "I'll remember this day as long as I live," he told them.

One day Ro was introduced to Eunice Finstrom, the daughter of a retired missionary to India. When she mentioned to him her father's longing for a good Indian dinner, Ro invited them to Mrs. Bartlett's house for "an authentic native meal." He fixed rice and chicken curry, some *puri,* the flat bread of his homeland, and split-pea *dal.*

The old missionary ate everything with great gusto, fondly recalling his missionary days on the Asian subcontinent. He enjoyed himself so much that Ro was glad he had invited them.

Another pleasant surprise came when Watkin Roberts journeyed from Toronto "just to see you, Rochunga." The old man was already seventy, and his leg seemed to drag more heavily than the year before. But his mind was sharp, and his heart warm.

By this time Ro had set up an improvised office in Mrs. Bartlett's basement. Mr. Young Man seemed pleased when he saw the pile of books and manuscripts spread across Ro's desk, where he had been revising the Hmar New Testament.

Slowly, Roberts eased himself into a chair. The old missionary's eyes still sparkled with purity and purpose. "I'm getting old, Rochunga," he sighed. "These legs of mine do not obey orders anymore." He tapped his lame leg with his cane. Then, he became more focused. "Rochunga, for almost forty years I've been praying for someone from the Hmars to carry on the work that God began with me among your people. I've come here to see if God might have said something to you."

It was hard to resist his invitation, but Ro realized that he was being asked to head an organization that was no organization at all. True, the missionary had kept the work that he had begun in India alive through the years. But it had no assets, no capital, board of directors or staff, not even a mailing list. All the Indo-Burma Pioneer Mission had was a group of native workers, who loved the Lord and had committed to serving him, plus an old man on the other side of the world, who wrote encouraging letters and sent what money he could.

"*Pu Tlangval,* I cannot say yes now. I have my studies to complete. And I *must* finish the Hmar Bible translation. It is a promise I must keep," Ro told him.

The light in the old man's eyes seemed to go out. It was like the dimming of a lamp. His shoulders drooped, and his head bowed. It was obvious that he had hoped for a different answer.

After a moment he cleared his throat and spoke softly. "Rochunga, you know how much I love India and your people, for whom I've given my life. I was not permitted to live with them at Senvon, but in my heart I have been dwelling with them for nearly fifty years."

"I am not turning my back on you, sir. I *will* truly pray about it, *Pu Tlangval,*" Ro promised. Roberts seemed content with that.

"My prayers will follow you, Rochunga. I will ask God to make the way plain and to help you clear these other commitments so you can seriously pray about my request."

\*       \*       \*

144

In Toronto, some weeks later, Ro reported to Watkin Roberts. He had considered Mr. Young Man's proposal carefully and prayerfully, for he did not want to hurt the beloved missionary.

"As I finish the translation work, I will be speaking in churches. I will tell those who wish to help India to send money to you. We can build up a small mailing list, and if the Lord so leads, I can become the organizing secretary in a year or two."

"But I want *you* to take over and build the mission," Roberts interrupted. "I can wait, but what about the multitudes of India?"

Ro could see that they had a common purpose and love for India and its people.

"Then let us both pray for God to show us the way," Ro told him.

# Chapter Ten
## *God's Treasure: Lalrimawi*

A letter came from Ro's brother-in-law, Luoia, in India, interesting for its timing so soon after his meeting with Watkin Roberts. Luoia wrote, "I am now chief of the village of Sielmat. Would you like twenty acres of land for your missionary work?"

This was exciting! Sielmat was adjacent to Churachandpur, one of the fastest growing towns in northeast India, and it was connected with the state capital by a good road. It was only thirty-five miles from the Imphal airport, which had a daily flight to Calcutta and two flights a week to New Delhi. Sielmat would be a much better location for a mission headquarters than either Senvon or Phulpui. And twenty acres would be enough for Ro to build a church, boarding school, hospital, and even a college!

Next Ro got special permission from the Indian government for Watkin Roberts to visit the northeast tribal area. Persuading Mr. Young Man that he should go and personally investigate the Sielmat site for a mission operation was no problem. For more than forty years the former missionary had longed to see his beloved tribal friends.

From village to village swift Hmar runners carried the glad message: "Mr. Young Man is returning!" There was wild excitement throughout the land, for by this time the majority of the tribe had become Christians.

Finally his plane landed at Imphal airport, and a large delegation was on hand to greet him. As Watkin Roberts limped down the stairs from the plane, he was greeted with a loud cheer as the Hmar people practically mobbed the plane. Their first glimpse of his white hair made them awestruck. Their culture taught them to revere age and wisdom, and he was the perfect example of both.

Watkin Roberts came down the stairs of the plane slowly and was lifted by many eager hands onto a sedan chair, on which he was reverently carried to a jeep waiting to take him to Sielmat, some thirty-five miles away.

In Sielmat a pig was already roasting for a feast in his honor. The entire village gathered for the welcoming ceremony, and a local committee presented him with the special *puondum*. They draped the beautiful striped cloth as a robe over his shoulders. He was the first white man to be so honored.

The greatest thrill for Watkin Roberts, however, came when he saw the multitude of tribesmen bow in prayer to God before the feast began. To see so many transformed lives was his real honor.

The old man's eyes welled with tears of rejoicing and thanksgiving to God for giving him this experience while he was still alive. It validated the ministry that the missionary had had to leave behind, never knowing the results of his efforts.

Roberts would have liked to have visited Senvon village, where in response to Chief Kamkholun's invitation some forty-seven years earlier, he had first brought the gospel to the

Hmars. But for Roberts, a one hundred-mile hike was not possible; instead, he had to be content visiting villages that could be reached by the sedan chair carried by grateful pastors.

Traveling with Chawnga, Mr. Thanglung, and other Hmar church leaders, he kept hearing English words that had crept into the Hmar language: *Bible school, conference, committee, pastor, newspaper, Bible woman.* He was certain that most of the Hmars didn't even realize the origin of such words but accepted them as Hmar words. They had become part of their vocabulary, largely through the influence of the gospel.

At Lakhipur, Roberts attended the annual assembly of the church denomination that represented the majority of the Hmar Christians. In the years that had passed, his original five converts had become a far-flung assembly of well over one hundred church congregations, with thousands of members. He listened as the church leaders voted to merge the church administration with the new mission work to be established at Sielmat, and that also pleased him immensely.

Before ending his nostalgic journey, Mr. Young Man asked the church leaders what they thought of Rochunga becoming the leader of the church and mission in the United States. They were thrilled. "We have always felt that there was capable leadership within the tribe," one of the leaders told him.

To Roberts this was an understatement. As he looked around him and recalled the ceremony when all the churches and their leaders were represented, it was obvious to him that God could raise up a church without the help of white missionaries from the West. Roberts had often said in the West, "We must trust that the same Holy Spirit who is operative in us is also operative in them. He will guide them, teach them, correct them and inspire them to do his will." It was a message that got him in trouble with other mission leaders, but that was simply because he was so ahead of his time.

In fact, the times were changing. Native leadership would be the way of the future.

Watkin Roberts returned from his tour of Hmar churches and sought out Ro. "Your people have full confidence in you, Rochunga. You must not disappoint them."

"Both you and my Hmar people honor me," he said. "But I must finish my education and get the Hmar Bible ready for publication. That is the vision God gave to my father and to me, and it must be completed. I will organize a board and raise funds for the mission work in America."

\*      \*      \*

As soon as Ro returned to Wheaton in 1958, he began to push hard on the translation work. But in response to Watkin Roberts's plea, he organized the first board of directors for the Indo-Burma Pioneer Mission in America. He insisted that Watkin Roberts be listed as founding member, and the board installed Ro as executive director.

To help complete the translation of the Hmar Bible, he hired a typist for $1.00 an hour while he worked in the college library for $1.50 an hour. By that summer he felt the manuscript was ready to take to London for publication.

Ro celebrated the completion of the long and arduous task privately. There was no one with whom he could share his joy. It was at times like this that he thought of taking a wife but wondered how to find a young woman who could adapt to his hectic life and work. But now at least the New Testament translation was done.

Upon arrival in London, he took the Hmar New Testament, revised and polished, to Dr. Bradnock.

While in England, he visited with two sisters, daughters of Mr. Thanglung, who were in Great Britain to study nursing. As was the custom, the parents were thinking of a possible match between Ro and one of the sisters. He had been exchanging letters with one of them, Hnemi, but she had stopped writing. Ro visited her when he got to England, but their conversations never got beyond small talk.

Several days after this visit, Hnemi came to see him and confessed. "I must ask you to forgive me. Two months ago I met an American GI and fell in love with him. That's why I stopped writing to you.

"But it was a mistake," she admitted. "Paul broke up with me last week and left. I want you to consider a relationship with me again. I am very sorry."

After a long pause Ro realized he had no feelings for her. He responded with a quote from Shakespeare: "'The nest is warm, but the bird has flown.' I am sorry that things did not work out for you and Paul. Nor for us. But let us continue as friends, like brother and sister in the Lord."

He thought about the experience on the way home. *It must not be God's plan,* he told himself disappointedly. *Perhaps I am to remain a bachelor all my days.*

As he was returning one day from classes back in America, Ro picked up his mail from Mrs. Bartlett and found a copy of the Hmar Student Association magazine (which he had started as a student in Allahabad). He read it eagerly, enjoying the contact with his homeland. As he read a list of names of young Hmars who had passed their high school exams and were going on to college, he noticed a familiar name. Lalrimawi, was enrolled at St. Mary's College in Shillong, Assam.

*Rimawi—how do I know that name?* he wondered. Then he remembered. Rimawi was one of the girls he had taught English in 1953. Now she was studying at St. Mary's—no doubt the first girl from the Hmar tribe to go to college. Ro decided to write her a note of congratulations.

He sent a small gift along with the note. A gracious thank-you letter came back to Ro from Rimawi. In it she mentioned the English classes and told him how much his encouragement had meant to her.

Ro was prompted to write her again. He asked if she was having any problems as a Protestant attending a Roman Catholic college and offered his help in any way she might need.

The mail took several weeks for letters to be exchanged. Meanwhile Ro kept busy and was feeling low, partly because of the fatigue of long hours of study, work, and the energy-consuming efforts of trying to raise funds for the fledgling mission work in India.

One Saturday morning Ro awoke restless and unhappy. Like the beginning of the dismal monsoon season in his homeland, his future seemed to stretch endlessly before him. He began to doubt his work and all that he was doing. He felt sorry for himself in giving up his try for a political career, wondering if by now he might not be in Parliament, mingling with influential people, perhaps even being of more help to his people.

He sighed deeply and slipped down to his basement office. He tried to pray but had some difficulty concentrating. Lunchtime came, and still he prayed. Finally he went to get the mail.

As he sorted through the pieces, he was encouraged to see a letter from Rimawi. He sat down to read it carefully. It was written in English, not Hmar. Rimawi was taking him up on his offer to help in any way—she asked for his prayers. "My brother, Khuma, is taking his B.A. final exams. Please pray for him."

Then she went on: "You asked if I have problems. Yes. But I do not pray for an easy path and that all the barriers should be broken down for me. I only pray that God will give me the strength, in my weakness, to do his will, for he has said, 'My grace is sufficient for thee.'" Ro was so moved by her resolute faith and trust in God that he felt ashamed.

*Why should I feel discouraged?* he asked himself. He went to his room, combed his hair, and went out for lunch, strangely warmed by the letter from Rimawi.

Later he read her letters over and over. Although they had been corresponding for many months now, he tried to recall her face from the memory of those English classes but could recall only her luminous dark eyes smiling beneath smooth braids of black hair piled on her head.

A search of his files helped him find a photo of her that he had taken that summer, but the picture was over five years old. She looked like

a thousand other Hmar girls in their early teens.
By now she was nineteen. What would she look
like now?

\*       \*       \*

Ro received a letter from Bob Pierce: "Would you
like to join our World Vision team for a series of
summer pastors' conferences in Japan, Taiwan,
Singapore, Burma, and India? All your expenses
will be paid."

India! It had been four long years since he
had left India, and Ro eagerly looked forward to
returning to his homeland and seeing the
incredible green hills and beautiful valleys of
Manipur.

And maybe he could make a side trip to
Shillong in order to visit Rimawi. That was really
something exciting to look forward to! Ro was his
old self again—exuberant, optimistic, and carried
away with enthusiasm.

Adding to his excitement was the fact that
the galley proofs of the Hmar New Testament had
arrived from the British and Foreign Bible Society.
Proofing and correcting them was a delight. It
gave him such satisfaction to see his own
translation of God's Word at last being printed in
Hmar!

Within the month, Ro left to join the World
Vision team for the pastors' conference in Japan.
Fifteen hundred people came just to pray, share
in fellowship and testimonies, participate in Bible
study, and listen to inspiring teachers. Most of
them would have been unable to attend without
World Vision's financial assistance. The Americans on the program included Bob Pierce, Dr.

Paul S. Rees, Dr. Richard Halverson, Dr. Larry Ward, Kurt Kaiser (musician) and others.

Ro spoke one evening, thrilling them with his testimony and bringing tears to the eyes of the usually stoic Asians. Afterward Bob Pierce hugged him like a giant panda. "You were great, brother!" he said enthusiastically. "You really encouraged them. You know, Ro, as an Asian, you can reach them in a way that we Westerners can't."

The final pastors' meeting was in Calcutta, and Chawnga came down for that conference. When it ended, Ro and his father left at once for the hills of Manipur. What a welcome he received! There was feasting and thanksgiving to God, with hundreds of people coming to Sielmat to hear him preach. Then, when he announced that the Hmar New Testament would soon be ready, a loud cheer went up from the crowd.

Later, Chawnga and Daii were anxious to have a private conversation with their "celebrity" son.

"Is everything well with you?" Ro asked his parents politely.

They assured him that they were both in good health. "My son, it is you we are concerned about," Daii said gently. "You will soon be thirty-one years old and you are still unmarried. There are too many problems for a single man in the ministry, especially one who is now the head of a mission."

"M-my mother," Ro stammered, feeling like a ten-year-old. "As head of a mission, with so many responsibilities, how can I go around looking over girls in the short time that I have here? It is impossible."

But Daii was determined. And she surprised her son with her next words. "Have you met a college girl named Lalrimawi? She is now studying in Shillong, but she came here last summer for the student conference. We liked her very much."

He did not tell his mother that he had been in correspondence with Rimawi. He tried another approach. "But Shillong is three hundred miles away!" he told her. Yet to himself he thought, *If God would work it out, I would truly like to meet Rimawi.*

Ro hadn't told his parents that he had already invited Rimawi to come to Sielmat during the Puja vacation in mid-October. Schools closed for the two weeks of that Hindu festival, and he could see her then. But, regrettably, a letter came from Rimawi saying that while she appreciated the invitation, she did not feel it would be proper for her to come.

Then, a week later a beautiful hand-knit sweater from Rimawi arrived in the mail, along with a note indicating her wish that he would visit Shillong before his return to America.

Ro really wanted to visit Shillong, but as he had told his mother, it was three hundred miles away, and how could he? He'd already agreed to take a month-long tour of interior villages, beginning with Lakhipur in November. That tour would last until just before Christmas. And since he was scheduled to return to the U.S. in January, there was just no way to fit it into his schedule.

Then a letter came from Reverend Culshaw, the translation secretary of the Bible Society in Bangalore, inviting him to take part in a Bible translators' conference *in Shillong* the first part of November. Could he come?

It seemed like a miracle. He reorganized his mission tour and found that he could still cover most of the itinerary following the translators' conference.

When Ro arrived at the Pinewood Hotel in Shillong, the desk clerk told him that some students were planning a reception in his honor in the tea room. He went expectantly to the tea, but Rimawi, the student he most wanted to see, was not there.

Troubled, he hurried over to St. Mary's College as soon as the tea was over, but the gates were already closed. He stood there in the dusk, looking through the bars at the dormitory. So near yet so far.

He returned the next day and asked for Rimawi. Taking a seat in the large, austere parlor, he waited impatiently.

After an eternity—actually only a few minutes—he caught sight of a beautiful young woman, wearing a tribal cloth skirt and white embroidered blouse approaching. He rose to his feet in recognition.

She smiled shyly, and his heart skipped a beat. *This is the one*, he told himself intuitively. *I know that this is the one.*

The nuns had given them permission to spend five to ten minutes together, but the time stretched into half an hour. As they talked, Ro felt that she was a girl he could trust. But in two months he'd be twelve thousand miles away, and the thought of leaving this soft-voiced, sensitive girl tore at his heart.

*I must be bold and trust that she will understand,* he decided. So he abruptly declared, "I came here to see if you might be God's choice for me."

He caught the surprise that flickered in her dark eyes and the flush of color in her delicate cheeks as she gazed at the floor shyly.

"I leave the country in January. Will you please pray about it?" he asked her.

She looked away shyly and whispered, "Yes, I will pray."

"Please pray *soon.* The time is so short."

Rimawi dropped her eyes once more.

*Have I spoken too boldly or too hastily?* Ro wondered. Then she looked up, and her soft smile was reassuring.

"We have already talked past the time," she observed.

He glanced at his watch. The time had simply flown. He rose to leave. "Would you mind if I called you Mawii (meaning 'beautiful one')? It is so appropriate."

She modestly blushed again, then nodded her approval.

The next day Ro was occupied at the translators' conference, but he still made time for his pressing personal business.

Also in keeping with Hmar custom, he sent a delegate (a distant cousin who happened to be in Shillong) with a formal letter to Rimawi to discuss a possible marriage. Ro also sent her a warm, encouraging letter he wrote during free moments.

"I am sitting by a warm, flickering fire thinking about you. I would be the happiest man in this hemisphere if our loving Father would join the two of us as one," Ro said in one of the letters.

His messenger returned to report, "She is definitely praying over the matter and says she will give you an answer on Sunday."

Sunday was their first real date, and Ro took her canoeing on Ward Lake in front of the Pinewood Hotel. The sky had never seemed bluer, the sun brighter, nor the water clearer as he paddled on the smooth lake.

Blind to the curious onlookers on the shore, Mawii read to him from *Tlangchar Tuihnar (Mountain Spring)*, the devotional book he had written. The words, as Mawii read them, were so captivating and inspirational that it was hard to believe that he had written them himself.

They each sat back in the canoe and drifted along on the water, neither bringing up the subject that was at the top of the agenda.

Finally Ro could hold back no longer; his heart was pounding. "Mawii, will you marry me?" he blurted out.

Mawii put the book down and looked at him directly. She spoke slowly, carefully. "I have been praying about it, and even as I prayed, I found myself praising the Lord for having brought about this miracle.

"Many long years ago, when I saw you at the school at Pherzawl, where you came to teach English during your school break, I prayed that if I were ever to marry, it would be someone like Rochunga. I wanted to marry a man who loved God as you do, but I never thought it was possible that it would be *you*.

158

"Now I see how the Lord has worked his plan to bring us together, and I will be happy to be your wife.

"But I must have the consent of my parents and the approval of my family," she added.

Ro sent a telegram the next morning to his mother and father in Sielmat: Being in the way the Lord led me. Stop. Letter follows.

Ro also notified his American friend, Dr. Bob Pierce, and Watkin Roberts. Roberts wrote back, expressing a view about the name of Ro's bride-to-be, which he had shared with Pierce, "She must come from a wonderful Christian home to have a name like Rimawi."

As he left Shillong the next day, for the first time ever Ro felt the bittersweet ache of romantic loneliness. But his heart was full and satisfied. He had found *the* girl, and she had said yes.

The scheduled tour of villages began as planned in Lakhipur, where Ramlien, Ro's older brother, was a pastor. After the Hmar custom, Ro sent Ramlien and K. Luoia to Khawlien village, where Mawii's parents lived. They carried a blue-and-white cloth (to signify a pleasant home) and a hoe (a symbol of peace and contentment). The two men were to obtain permission from Mawii's parents for her to marry Ro. Then they were to take the news to him in Senvon where Ro would be by that time.

Ramlien understood his brother's anxious desire to know the results of their visit, so he sent a signal by lights across the valley from Khawlien: "We are successful!"

Ro was excited and hoped Mawii could make arrangements so that they could be married and go back to America together in January.

# Chapter Eleven
## *To America—with Faith and $26*

At four o'clock on New Year's Day, 1959, Ro was standing near the altar of the William Carey Baptist Church, smiling broadly as he watched his bride floating down the aisle toward him.

She glanced his way and smiled back at him. Their eyes locked. *She looks like a princess,* he thought. *A beautiful Hmar princess. And she is my bride!*

Mawii took her place at Ro's side as Pastor Corlett spoke the solemn words of the marriage ceremony. When the kindly minister paused, Ro realized it was time for him to say, "I do." Then the groom listened as Mawii's soft, clear voice repeated the words.

"I now pronounce you man and wife," the pastor declared. A small reception was held in the church gardens. Church members, who knew Ro as a student, showered them with good wishes. The couple spent their wedding night at the Baptist mission home.

The next day the newlyweds boarded a train for Madras, where they attended the Asian Christian Youth Congress. From there the couple traveled to Vellore for a post-Congress crusade, where Ro substituted for an American evangelist who was ill. Vellore is famous for its Christian medical training center.

Ro was humorously introduced as the "great honeymoon preacher," but he felt more like a honeymoon breaker. He wished it could have been possible to take his bride on a romantic trip alone somewhere, perhaps to see the Taj Mahal, but he was pleased by her gracious attitude. It was obvious that the Lord had not only brought them together but had given them a wonderful love for one another. And they both wished to serve him.

From Vellore, the couple traveled back to northeast India. At Sielmat Ro presented his new bride to his family. Ro explained to his mother how God had led in this choice and told her how they had also followed the Hmar customs in making the arrangements. Ro remarked about how beautifully suited they were to one another and for God's service.

Daii smiled. "You are truly what we call *pathien samsui*," she said, using the Hmar expression meaning "Those whom God has tied together by braids in the hair."

Ro grinned. "In America, the expression is 'A marriage made in heaven.'"

Mawii was pleased by the customs and traditions of their Hmar friends and relatives in making their marriage a happy event. But she was excited and happy when she was told that her seventy-five-year-old father had come to wish the couple his blessing by walking five days through the rugged mountains and jungles.

"Your brothers told me that Rochunga was a good man and would make you a fine husband," her aging father said. "But I wanted to see with my own eyes."

Mawii felt the depth of his love, and she was choked with emotion when he told her, "It is very hard for your mother and me to think of our youngest child going to the far side of the world, where we may never see her again."

Ro listened and was deeply touched by the dear man's love for his daughter. He explained their plans for the future: "Since Mawii's college exams are not going to be held until February, we have postponed our departure to America. We will have time to come to your village so Mawii can properly say good-bye to her mother."

"That will please her very much," his father-in-law said with a smile. "We will have another celebration, and you can meet all of your new relatives."

When Ro and Mawii arrived in Khawlien a few weeks later, they found a huge feast had been prepared in their honor. Mawii was thrilled to receive the chest her parents had made for her, filled with beautiful hand-woven cloths. It was quite a practical gift, too, since Mawii had given most of her Hmar blouses away to her new husband's relatives, again according to tradition. Ro was particularly impressed with Ruolneikhum, his new brother-in-law, whom everyone called Khuma. He had been studying for his master's degree at Allahabad University.

"I am planning to enter government service after I finish my master's dissertation," Khuma explained to Ro.

"Why not come and help us start the new Christian high school?" Ro invited. "We really need you. And you can work on your dissertation while teaching at the new school."

Khuma agreed, and when they arrived back in Sielmat, he began planning the curriculum and looking for teachers. Ro worked with his brother-in-law for several days and then set about starting nine village schools, including one in Khawlien with some funds raised through the Indo-Burma Pioneer Mission. Only the lack of extra funds kept him from establishing more.

The time soon came for Mawii to take her college examinations. In order for her to receive credit for her two years of college work a passing grade was required. She was a bit apprehensive, however, since in her mind she had not been studying enough since their marriage.

Ro accompanied her to Imphal, where the results could be obtained. When results were announced, he swelled with pride. "Why, you did even better than I did!" he exclaimed.

A letter arrived from Reverend Corlett, pastor of the Carey Baptist Church, announcing that Bob Pierce was coming to India and wanted to meet with Ro in Calcutta. The young groom traveled there, met with Pierce, and introduced his new bride.

"Ro, you must come back to the U.S. and finish your work," Pierce told him. He was told that World Vision would help him with his travel expenses.

As they made plans to come to America, Ro discovered that the Indian government foreign exchange regulations prohibited them from taking any money out of India. All they were allowed was sixty-five rupees (about thirteen dollars each in American money).

He and Mawii prayed about it. "You decide," she told him, "and we will go."

They flew by way of an overnight stop in London, where most of their money was spent on lodging and small meals.

\*      \*      \*

Their itinerary for North America took them to Canada first. It was a joyous occasion for Ro when he said to Watkin Roberts at the Toronto airport, "I am pleased to introduce my wife, Mawii."

Mr. Young Man immediately took her to his heart as a daughter and insisted that they stay a few days before continuing on to Chicago. Ro also used the time to report all the details to Roberts about the beginnings of the new work of the Indo-Burma Pioneer Mission in northeast India. But he did not tell Roberts that he had no money and that the Indian government had allowed them only the equivalent of thirteen dollars each on leaving the country.

On June 6, 1959, the couple finally arrived in Chicago. When they reached Midway Airport, however, Ro didn't have enough for a bus or taxi ride to Wheaton. In fact, all he had left was a quarter. Ro decided to use it to call Mrs. Bartlett and see if she could come to the airport to pick them up. Local calls were a dime, but the operator said Wheaton was a long distance call, and it cost thirty-five cents. Ro told her all he had was a quarter, but the operator was insistent.

Ro said, "I will put in the twenty-five cents and send you another twenty-five cents in the mail." Still the operator would not place the call. He tried looking in the coin slots of the other nearby phones but found nothing.

Ro put the quarter back in his pocket and prayed, *Lord, you do not need a telephone to speak to people. Please tell Mrs. Bartlett to come for us.*

He went back to the curbside, where Mawii was waiting with their luggage. "Is Mrs. Bartlett coming?"

"Yes," Ro replied with as much conviction as he could muster. "It takes nearly an hour to drive from Wheaton to the airport. We must wait."

An hour later the couple was still sitting on the grass outside the terminal. It was pleasant enough, except for the exhaust of the cars pulling up to discharge their passengers.

Ro glanced at his watch while silently praying. Then he heard his name being called. "Rochunga! Ro! Is that you?"

It was Mrs. Bartlett! In the car beside her was her grown daughter.

Ro walked over to the car. "Yes," he replied with a broad smile, "it is me." And he proudly introduced his new bride. Then he said, "I am so glad you came, Mrs. B."

"Well, I remember getting a letter some time ago that had your itinerary in it, and my daughter had never seen a jetliner, so we simply decided to come to Midway Airport."

"God sent you to get us. May we ride back to Wheaton with you?"

Mrs. Bartlett drove the couple back to Wheaton, but since she'd already rented out Ro's old room, he planned to check with Wheaton College to see if he could arrange for housing—for an apartment that he could rent without having to pay a deposit.

While they were at Mrs. Bartlett's house, a phone call came for Ro.

"Ro, this is Jim Watt. I just took a chance on calling there, hoping someone could help me find you—and that you weren't still in India.

"I need your help," his friend said to Ro. "I just found out that our missions conference speaker is ill, and I need someone to preach on Friday, Saturday, and Sunday. Can you do it?"

Ro agreed to help, and on the final night, the church took a love offering. The $147.29 was enough for an apartment! There was even some money left over to buy food staples.

Back into the routine of Wheaton, Ro enjoyed the pleasure of introducing his bride to all his friends. It now seemed so natural and pleasant to have her with him; it was as if a void in his life had now been filled.

Mawii was impressed by the friendly, open, and frank Americans. She was a little shy about her English, although everyone encouraged her by telling her that she spoke the language quite well. The church services were a distinct blessing to her, after years of only private devotions in the Catholic college.

*       *       *

One day Ro dropped by to see one of the Indo-Burma Pioneer Mission board members, John Jess, who was the prominent radio preacher for *Chapel of the Air*. He reported to Jess about his recent tour of India and the progress among the Hmars. He told Jess about the enthusiasm of the tribal church leaders to start more schools and build a strong mission base, which in turn led to more and more churches being planted. "With nationals telling other nationals," Ro told him, "all of northeast India can be evangelized." Ro carefully explained the plan, then declared optimistically, "I must enlist the help of all the Christians in America."

Jess chuckled at Ro's determination. "Well, just how are you going to get around to see everybody?"

"I'll start with these two strong legs!" Ro replied with enthusiasm.

"Those legs won't take you very far. This is a huge country."

Ro's eyes shone with determination. "They are strong enough. I will walk from house to house until I have knocked on every door in Wheaton. Then I will go to Glen Ellyn and Lombard and—"

"Whoa—just a minute," Jess interrupted. "Why don't you let me put a little speed to your faith? Go over to Madsen's used car lot. When you get there, pick out any car you like. I'll pay for it."

Excited as a schoolboy, Ro dashed down to the lot and looked over the autos lined up on display. He placed his hands on a shiny, late-model Plymouth. *Lord, is this the one?* he prayed. There was no answer.

He moved to another, a beautiful two-door coupe. *Is it this one, Lord?* No answer. So he moved to another, and another, praying over each car that he came to. Finally, he came to an old 1952 Mercury, far from being the newest car on the lot. In fact, it was with a little reluctance that Ro prayed, *Lord, is it this one?* But this time an inner voice seem to confirm his choice. *It's yours! It's yours!*

By this time a salesman from the used car lot had noticed the strange foreigner placing his hands on his cars. "Hey, what are you doing?" he called to Ro.

"I am looking for my car," Ro replied.

"Your what?"

"My car. This one. What is the price?"

The salesman told him it would cost him $275 and went on to extol its many virtues, lifting the hood to show off the engine.

Ro offered him $175, saying, "This is my car." The salesman began to haggle but Ro had perfected the art of haggling as a trader just after the war. However, this time he did not haggle. He just shook his head every time the dealer gave his counter-offer. The salesman first came down to $250, then $240, $230 and $225. Seeing Ro was firm, the man came down in price by tiny increments. Still each time Ro shook his head.

Exasperated, the used car dealer barked out one more price. "All right," he said, "I'll sell it for $175."

This time Ro nodded. "I'll take it. Now I will get the money. How shall the check be made out?"

John Jess was surprised that Ro had picked out one of the cheapest cars on the lot, but Ro insisted it was the one that God wanted him to have. Jess gave him the check and helped him with the title and license papers, then Ro was on his way home.

(Ro put over 100,000 miles on that old Mercury, driving it across the country and all over town, until one day it was struck by a drunk driver who paid him $150 for damages. Ro junked the car for another $35 and made $10 over the purchase price!)

Ro then rented a small upstairs room on Main Street for just $25 a month that became the Indo-Burma Pioneer Mission's first office. Here he compiled in a small dime-store composition book the mission's first mailing list—114 names.

Ro and Mawii worked together in getting out their first prayer letter. A friend let Ro mimeograph the letter at his office in Wheaton and Ro and Mawii folded the letters and hand-addressed and stamped each letter.

The two of them prayed for the letters and dropped them into the mailbox. The event was more than the start of their organization—it was the beginning of their lifetime together, not just in marriage, but in ministry. Putting the letters in the mail for the first time was a genuine thrill. It was just as exciting when the funds began to trickle in.

Meanwhile Mawii enrolled in summer school while Ro took to the road, driving over ten thousand miles across the Midwest in the old Mercury that summer. He presented his idea, a new concept that captured the imagination of church mission leaders: partnership between Americans and nationals. Ro created the slogan, "Nationals telling nationals the good news of Jesus Christ," as a means of communicating this new concept.

"Everyone knows that the day of the foreign missionary in India is fading," Ro told various church mission conference audiences. "I am not anti-missionary—after all, it was a missionary, Watkin Roberts, who brought the gospel to my tribe. But Americans are no longer allowed into India as missionary preachers and teachers. The foreign mission force drops every year as missionaries retire, while at the same time India's population continues to grow.

"Most members of our tribe are now Christians. We have hundreds of young men and women willing to become missionaries themselves to other tribes. But we are poor and unable to train and equip them and to send all of them.

"Remember, a national Christian does not need to raise support for passage; he is already there. He does not need expensive equipment or language training. He speaks the language and is already acquainted with the customs of the people. He cannot be expelled because he is not a foreigner.

"So we ask for your prayers and financial partnership in our program of nationals training and telling other nationals. Ten dollars will pay the tuition of a Bible college student for a month; forty dollars will support a pastor, a missionary, or an evangelist; one hundred dollars will operate an entire village school; a thousand dollars will build a two-room school or a small church." (Today the cost is one hundred-fifty dollars for a pastor or missionary; three thousand dollars for a school with teachers, and a minimum of ten thousand dollars to build a two-room school or small church.)

Wherever Ro spoke, he added names and addresses of interested supporters and friends to his growing mailing list.

Late that summer he returned to Wheaton, but a "secret" that the couple shyly had not shared with anyone was becoming apparent— Mawii was expecting a baby, so she did not enroll for the fall semester.

Ro was ecstatic at the prospect of his fatherhood. When he went out on speaking engagements, though, he became very lonely because Mawii was unable to accompany him.

When he returned from one speaking engagement, he was awakened by Mawii while it was still dark. She whispered urgently, "My time has come."

Ro dressed quickly and rushed outside into the cold November morning. The old Mercury got them to the hospital without a great margin of time to spare. An hour and a half after their arrival, the baby, whom the adoring parents thought was the most beautiful creature they'd ever seen, was born. The nurses smiled as Ro's bright eyes and face cheered the entire wing. The enchanted parents named him Paul Rozarlien. They felt he should have both a biblical name and a Hmar name, and the one they chose meant "God's treasure reaching out."

On the day that Paul was born, Mawii had been reading Psalm 139:14, and she was struck by the reality of the words, "I am fearfully and wonderfully made."

The birth of their son brought an added sense of completeness to their marriage and love for each other.

All in all, this had been quite a year! First, to begin the year, he had married Mawii. Then, when they were still in India, he had started nine new mission schools. When he returned to America, Ro had opened the Indo-Burma Pioneer Mission office in Wheaton, acquired a car, and begun barnstorming across the Midwest, stirring up interest in the fledgling mission work. And now he had a son!

The couple began the new year with an unbounded enthusiasm for what their God would accomplish. Since Ro and Mawii were in America on student visas, they both had to continue their schooling. So Ro attended graduate study classes at Northern Illinois University, a seventy-mile roundtrip every day, thinking that a master's degree in education from a U.S. university would be more beneficial for the educational projects Ro had planned for India than a theology degree. Meanwhile Mawii enrolled at Wheaton College.

But Ro's heart was more in the mission than in the classroom. He continued driving the old Mercury to scheduled speaking engagements nearly every weekend.

When summer came they rigged up a bassinet in the backseat of the old car and drove to Washington, D.C., stopping at many churches along the way to tell the story of the Hmars, meeting more people, and all the while adding to their mailing list. They returned to Wheaton wilted and exhausted but content in God's blessing of their ministry. Then they discovered another blessing—Mawii was expecting a second child.

The couple had worked hard during their second full year in America, and the mission income had quadrupled through their efforts; the year-end audit showed that they had taken in $40,971.17, compared to $9,643.90 the previous year. The results of their mission work in India had increased similarly. High school and Bible institute enrollments had gone up dramatically, and the number of village schools they started had doubled.

A few days later Ro was leading a seminar discussion at the university when a receptionist opened the door to the classroom and asked, "Is there someone here named Pudaite?"

Ro waved at her.

"You've just had a son born at St. Charles hospital."

Ro quickly wrapped up the discussion with whatever decorum he could muster and sped to the hospital—over a half hour away.

At home, Mawii's water bag had broken and it had frightened her. She prayed urgently, *Lord, what shall I do?* An inner voice told her to phone her doctor. She had dialed the number and explained what had happened. The doctor told her, "I'll be right over. Just take it easy."

But Mawii worried about the little toddler, Paul, and how to care for him if she suddenly had to go to the hospital. She prayed again for guidance, and insight came to her quickly. Mawii dialed the number of twelve-year-old Donna, who had taken care of Paul on other occasions.

Donna's father had answered the phone, and when Mawii explained the situation, said, "Of course. I'll drive her right over." While Mawii waited for the sitter, the doctor arrived and told her that her labor was too far advanced to wait any longer.

Donna and her father had arrived just as Mawii was packing a few things to take to the hospital. The doctor drove her to Delnor Hospital in St. Charles, talking all the way in order to take her mind off the contractions.

She was taken instantly into the delivery room. John Lalnunsang (his Hmar name means "the life of the Lord is greatest") was born shortly after Mawii and the doctor arrived at the hospital.

Truly, God had been very good to them.

# Chapter Twelve
## *The Dream Fulfilled*

The British and Foreign Bible Society sent a cable to Ro in December 1960 that the Hmar New Testaments were coming off the press. A few days later a special translator's copy arrived. As he opened the package, he took out the book and held it reverently in front of him, patting its black buckram cover.

Tears welled up in his eyes, and his mind went way back to his childhood. He remembered his father's voice telling of the need for someone to translate the Bible into the Hmar language. "We know that with God's help you can do it," Chawnga had encouraged him as a boy.

And he recalled his mother's words, "My hands will take up the hoe until you receive your degree!"

They had sacrificed so much so that he could take on the task; he felt a bit guilty that they were not here with him to bask in this moment of sincere gratitude to God and deep personal accomplishment.

It did not take long for the news to travel to northeast India announcing the end of the long "drought." *The Bibles are here!*

The printed Hmar New Testaments began to arrive, crates and crates of them, with five thousand copies in the first printing.

Thousands of Hmars thronged around the Sielmat mission headquarters building for a joyous feast of thanksgiving and to receive their own copies of the precious Book.

No one was happier than Chawnga, but he had regrets that Ro was not present to see the joy on the faces of the people.

Within six months the entire first printing was sold out, and an order for a second five thousand copies was placed.

Meanwhile, word came that the walls of the new high school building had been erected, but no corrugated steel roofing sheets were available anywhere. And the monsoons would be coming soon. Ro was busily trying to meet this pressing need.

Raising support for the growing work was a continual problem. The number of Christian workers now being supported by the mission had already passed one hundred, each requiring twenty-five dollars or more for monthly support. It was a modest amount by American standards, but it was a sizable sum for Ro to raise every month.

One month they were forty dollars short of meeting the total when it was time to mail the check to India. Ro put off mailing the check as long as he could, praying that the Lord would provide the full amount.

Two hours later a young student friend, John Arnold, stopped by the office on his lunch break. He pulled an envelope from his pocket and handed it to Ro. "For the work in India," he said simply. Inside were four ten-dollar bills.

Most of the support came from such people. An Illinois widow sent twenty-five cents a month; a thirteen-year-old California girl sent a dollar at a time from her baby-sitting earnings; an Iowa teenager sold greeting cards and sent a tithe of his sales income. A pastor and his wife figured they would spend fifty-seven dollars on Christmas gifts and sent half that amount for missions.

In India the Hmar Christians were every bit as generous. Almost all of the farmers gave a tithe of their small farm crops. Churches placed *thinghuon* (containers for firewood) on every trail leading into the villages so that women carrying firewood could drop one stick from each load into them. When full, the contents were sold and the proceeds given to church and mission projects.

When Khuma, Mawii's brother, came to Wheaton College Graduate School and later to Moody Bible Institute for further study, he handed over the mission work in India to Rev. Lalthankhum "Lal" Sinate.

It was encouraging to Ro to realize how many more tribesmen were becoming well educated and trained for leadership. Khuma and Lal had become Ro's most trusted and capable lieutenants. Either one, he felt, could hold the work in India together. When Ro's longtime dream of a Christian college was about to be realized, Khuma returned to Sielmat to be its principal.

The growing maturity and independence of the Hmar church was very pleasing to Ro, but it was not without internal friction. It was now late 1964, nearly five years since they had left India, and Ro thought it would be a good time for them to take a furlough back home.

The Hmars greeted them with a huge reception. Paul and John were the center of interest and were soon playing with their many cousins and picking up Hmar words, while their busy parents were taking part in the ceremonies to open the Sielmat Christian Hospital. The modest single-room, one-cot facility was the forerunner of a growing medical ministry to follow. The medical student, now *Doctor* Lal Puoklien, whom Ro and Mawii had supported through medical school, came to be its first doctor. The hospital also had a laboratory technician and a pharmacist.

Mawii, whose father had passed away when she was in America, was especially happy to spend time with her widowed mother while in India. "My mother," she said quietly, "I have a special secret to share with you. We are going to have another child. Ro and I would like for you to name this baby."

Her aging mother spent a few moments in silent contemplation. Then she announced, "The baby's name is to be Lalsangpui, meaning 'the Lord is supremely great.'"

Ro spent most of their four-month Indian furlough traveling, talking, praying, planning, and counseling. He encouraged the mission and the emerging Hmar churches to become autonomous and more independent. He wanted to stay for the church assembly, when new leaders would be elected and the church would move toward a separate identity, along with a new constitution, but he felt the need to return to America; donations were down in his absence.

Back in Wheaton, Ro mailed his resignation as president of the Hmar church, which was really an association of over one hundred churches, which they had started under the auspices of the Indo-Burma Pioneer Mission. But to his surprise, Ro was once again nominated and returned to the office of president of both organizations—the church and the mission.

The new independent church took over the bookstore, the preparation of literature, and part of the evangelism and other church-related activities formerly done by the mission. The mission continued to run the schools and the hospital and fund some of the national workers, whom the church could not yet support.

Then it was time for Ro and Mawii's third child to be born. They gave her the biblical name of Mary and, in accordance with the wishes of Mawii's mother, the Hmar name of Lalsangpui.

"Mother must have known this child would be a girl," Mawii laughed, "for she did not choose any boy's name." That was fine with Ro, because his heart had been set on a girl, and he was deeply content to finally have a daughter.

Their work seemed to be rolling along with God's blessing and provision. In the late 1960s the Board of Directors of Indo-Burma Pioneer Mission voted unanimously to change its name to Partnership Mission, which was more in keeping with their philosophy.

Later, Partnership Parents was started as a program that could meet the needs of poor children. Partnership Parents paired American and Canadian "foster parents" with Hmar Christian families who had opened their homes to impoverished and orphaned children in India to youngsters who would otherwise likely perish, be abandoned, or have no chance for an education.

Ro enlisted American sponsors to send twelve dollars monthly, which the mission sent overseas. The money provided housing, food, clothing, medical care, and a Bible-based education. (Today the Partnership Parents' sponsor support is twenty-one dollars monthly.)

The initial impetus for the program came when northeast India faced a number of severe famines resulting from serious crop failures and weather disasters that hit the area. It quickly grew as more and more "partnership parents" began to help.

Partnership Mission saw the program as the means of not only saving lives of the little ones in need but of getting its future Christian leaders, missionaries, and pastors by giving hundreds of children a Bible-based education.

Churches and individuals could become partners also by helping provide monthly support for native Indian pastors, evangelists, teachers, missionaries, doctors and nurses, and other dedicated Christian workers who were supported by Partnership Mission.

"Our biggest problem now is success," Ro told his board. "The college needs more buildings. Our little twenty-five-bed hospital must be enlarged. We have more workers in need of support and the number of orphans and needy children who need our help continues to grow."

Ro traveled to more churches, taking his growing family with him, and often they'd prepare an Indian meal for a church and feed hundreds of people. These events helped the organization to grow even more.

The work seemed to be gathering more momentum as it went along, and the income increased as a result of their efforts. Yet there were problems festering in northeast India about which Ro knew nothing. Finally, Khuma felt it was necessary to tell Ro about the troubles and get him to return to India at once.

# Chapter Thirteen
## *Another Tryst with Destiny*

Since the early 1950s neighboring tribes of the Hmars had been pushing for independence from India. They felt that there were enough differences between the tribal people and the rest of India's multitudes that warranted their own separate nation.

There were nearby precedents—East and West Pakistan had been created by the British some ten years earlier in response to similar logic. The Muslims of twin areas of Pakistan wanted to partition themselves from Hindu India.

In northeast India these dissidents asked for help from Western democracies to arm them for a major rebellion and secession.

But the foreign nations ignored them, so one rebel leader—blasting the countries who had sent them missionaries—lashed out, "They told us how to go to heaven, but they cannot help us get to the UN. Now we must turn to the East."

Two thousand young Nagas crossed the border into China to receive arms and guerilla training from the communist Chinese. Their return to northeast India in 1967 shook the usually tranquil mountains. In lightning quick response, the government in New Delhi declared the entire area "sensitive" and off-limits to foreign visitors.

Since the Hmars were loyal to their Indian government, they became the prime targets for subversion by the communist-inspired rebels.

Slowly, quietly, undercover agents, trained by the Chinese, worked themselves into positions of respect and influence in the Hmar society.

The rebellion was first kindled in the surrounding areas, then it ignited closer to home. Sielmat itself became a target for subversion and unrest.

Khuma saw that it could destroy all that Ro and the others had worked for over the years, yet he didn't even dare to put such fears on paper when he wrote to Ro in America, asking him to quickly return to India.

When he got Khuma's distress call, Ro acted immediately. He took his family—Mawii, Paul, John, and even three-year-old Mary—and boarded a plane for New Delhi.

A few days later, Khuma and Chawnga met them at the Imphal airport and laid out the terrible news.

Khuma said, "Communist propaganda has the campus in an uproar. They are spreading false stories about you all over the area."

According to the rumors, Ro was said to be a CIA agent who had smuggled $5 million into the country; the rumormongers asked why he didn't share that money with the people. The bogus stories also claimed Ro had brought arms and ammunition to the China-Burma border for the rebels.

The communists painted the Christian evangelical workers in the area (along with Ro) as rebels and sympathizers to the rebel cause. And to those on the rebel side of politics, Ro was branded a traitor opposed to home rule. *Neither* was true, but if people accepted either one of the lies, his credibility was gone.

The tales were ridiculous, but where to start in refuting them? The communists were quite convincing, even if the accusations were bold lies. When they heard that Ro had come to clear up the matter, things only intensified.

Threatening letters began to arrive for Ro at the mission headquarters:

You will be skinned alive so that you feel pain until the moment you expire.

If you don't leave India, we will hang you upside down behind your house.

You will never leave Manipur on your two feet.

There were twenty-nine such letters in all. Clearly Ro had become a marked man. Two weeks later after he had gone into the city, he received information that over a hundred armed men had surrounded his house, boasting that they would kill him before the night was over.

He was concerned for the welfare of his family, who were inside the house, so he quickly reported the situation to the local police, but they said it would take them several hours to muster a force large enough to confront a hundred armed men.

Ro could not wait for the police chief to act—even if he could get the men, there was no assurance that they'd protect him. He had to get home to his family.

Driving over a mile without his headlights, he approached his home and pulled up outside before any of the men knew what was happening. He jumped from the car and raced inside. There he saw Mawii, his brother, his parents, and the children quietly sitting and having devotions. They were not even aware of the men outside.

As Ro joined his family, little Mary began singing a chorus from a hymn: "I Trust in God Wherever I May Be." Then they prayed for God's safety and for their enemies.

The long night passed without incident or any attempt at forced entry. They were wondering what had happened to the men, when Khuma arrived. "When I learned that you couldn't get police help," he said, "I organized our friends to protect you. Those men did not dare attack. They left in the night."

Their house was surrounded by would-be attackers three more times. Each time loyal friends, with the help now of local police, prevented violence. Some of those who had threatened him with death were arrested and put in jail, where they could do no harm.

When the local authorities got things under control, Ro and Mawii prepared to return to Wheaton. Before leaving, Ro spoke to a delegation of Hmars. "We must forgive our enemies," he urged them. "Let us seek reconciliation with those who were deceived by the rebels and communist agitators."

To give them an example, Ro went to the jail and asked for the release of those charged with his attempted murder. He told the officials, "They were merely the pawns of rebel ringleaders, who have fled. We still love them and forgive them. Please let them go. When they realize they have been deceived, when they know the truth, they will be for us."

Ro went to meet with Governor Baleshwar Prasad at his residence in Imphal.

"Rochunga, it is not over yet," the governor told him. "I have just received a communiqué from New Delhi. Someone has charged you with smuggling U.S. $5 million into India. It's the same rumor we've been trying to put down here, but now it's gathered strength. It's gone full circle and I'm told there's going to be a full government inquiry."

"That's fine," Ro said. "The charges are false. We have absolutely nothing to hide."

"My friend," said the governor, his face growing serious as he explained, "you don't know how these things work. A government inquiry can take *years*. And if you are charged and put in jail waiting for the case to come up, well, I know of cases that have taken up to *fifteen years*. You can't stay and be arrested to await the disposition of your case."

"What do you mean?"

"Since I know that you are blameless, that you are innocent of the charges being made, I can say this. For the sake of your family and children, Rochunga, you must leave the country until all of this is settled.

"Go home. Don't even tell your parents. Trust no one. But tomorrow, fly to Delhi, then leave the country."

Ro had no idea that the charges were so serious. Yet, although he knew his innocence would ultimately prevail, he also knew it might take many years of waiting—*in jail!*—for his case to come up.

Governor Prasad continued, "Send your luggage at night so no one sees it. After breakfast in the morning, take a leisurely drive back here to Imphal and meet me here.

"I'll get your airline tickets. When you get to the Imphal airport, you should send telegrams to friends or associates in Shillong and other areas, asking if you can visit them. This will throw off any suspicion in case these troublemakers are watching you."

"Such actions will make me feel as if I have really done something wrong," Ro told him.

The governor put his hand on Ro's shoulder. "Money smuggling is a terrible crime. We both know that you have not done it, but you can be arrested and imprisoned for fifteen years just waiting for justice. You simply cannot stay. You must fight this from abroad."

Reluctantly, Ro did as he was told. Telling only the two men he trusted implicitly, Khuma and Rev. Lal Sinate, he sent his luggage in the middle of the night to Imphal and left after breakfast to meet with Governor Prasad. The governor gave Ro the promised airline tickets and hugged him affectionately.

Two of Ro's friends went on ahead to the airport, where they ran into one of the key troublemakers, who watched as the two sent telegrams to Shillong and a few other areas asking if Ro might visit them.

The governor's foresight paid off. The troublemaker left the airport certain that Ro was flying to Shillong to visit.

By the time someone came from New Delhi to Manipur to ask about Ro, he was already back in the United States with his family.

An official government investigation of the entire affair did get under way. All of the mission's staff and employees were instructed to cooperate and make all the files, financial books, and correspondence available to the investigators. A full inquiry was conducted, in an effort to get to the bottom of the accusations.

The officials dug into every record, every file and every report of the mission's work. They examined its financial records, bank accounts, and books. In the end, they could not find even a *hint* of wrongdoing. Ro's reputation was at last officially cleared, and he could return to India.

As the officials closed their books on the whole episode, one of the government men said to Khuma and Lal, "We have never seen any organization that operates with such integrity and accomplishes so much with so little. Carry on!"

\*      \*      \*

Back in Wheaton, a call came from Watkin Roberts's daughter, Ruth. "Ro, Dad is dying. I believe it is his time. He's having a lot of pain and complications. He's ready to go."

The great missionary died before the Pudaite family got to Toronto, but a few days later they were present for the simple funeral services conducted by Dr. Oswald J. Smith. Ro briefly eulogized the missionary pioneer whose sacrifice in India had literally changed the course of history for his tribe by showing them the way to Christ.

Now nearly the entire tribe of one hundred and twenty thousand were Christians!

Ro and Mawii felt the finest way to pay tribute to his memory was to continue the work that Watkin Roberts had loved so much.

The entire family went "on the road" over the summer of 1970 on a twelve-thousand-mile journey through seventeen states. They cooked and served "thank you" Indian dinners for thousands of their loyal supporters in scores of churches.

By August, Ro's hay fever made him suffer, so he usually scheduled some vacation time when the family could go to northern Wisconsin, where a friend had offered a cabin, away from the ragweed pollen. This year, however, Mawii did not go with them. She had been asked to come back to India and organize the work of Partnership Parents and the Sielmat Christian Hospital. In her absence, Ro took care of the children.

They had driven only about a hundred miles on their way to northern Wisconsin when they had car trouble. Their small Volkswagen wouldn't run at all. Ro called a tow truck and gathered the children around him while the mechanic hooked up the tow chain.

He didn't know what to do. Should he rent a motel room and have the children be cooped up there while the mechanics worked on his car? Should they simply wait at the repair shop for them to do the work? Ro asked the children to pray about their dilemma. When it was little Mary's turn, she was quite specific.

"Dear God," she began, "we don't want to stay here. My brothers want to catch fish. And I do, too. Why don't you do something, God?"

When they finished praying, Ro called the manager of the local VW agency, where the car had been taken, and told him their problem.

The man told Ro, "Come right over. I'll give you a loaner to take up north. You can pick up your car when you come back."

It was as simple as that—and they were fishing by sundown. Ro learned never to doubt the faith of a child.

At year's end Ro gave his annual report to his board of directors. "This year has been our best year to date, despite the trouble in northeast India. Giving was up 40 percent from the previous year, from $147,000 to over $211,000 in 1970.

"The mission is now supporting 350 national missionaries. We also have sixty-five village schools in operation, a Christian high school, and the hospital.

"As you know, because of the political unrest in Manipur, we have had to shut down the college, but Khuma hopes that it will reopen soon.

"Twelve new churches have been started in Manipur and Assam, with over two thousand converts. Besides this, we have distributed a half million tracts and a quarter million copies of the Gospel of John among the hill tribes."

Ro was eagerly looking forward to the year ahead to give them even more opportunities. Yet, he wondered if the work could not more or less get along without him—if perhaps God had a larger role for him to fulfill. Then, coincidentally, a letter came in January:

The communist who has represented Manipur in Parliament has no chance of being reelected. If you will come and file as our candidate, you will be unopposed and we can assure your election as a member of Parliament.

Ro showed the letter to Mawii. With a big smile, he said, "Read this." He handed her the letter. He watched as her eyes widened in wonder.

"Oh, Ro!" she declared. "This is wonderful!" Then she looked up at him, and her face clouded. "B-but you aren't really considering doing it, are you? We'd have to give up our work here and return to India."

"Well," Ro said thoughtfully, "I could at least think about it. A member of Parliament. Why, I gave up on that dream years ago."

To Mawii's chagrin, Ro's eyes reflected more than just a superficial interest. He began privately asking different friends and board members what they thought. Everyone was encouraging. It seemed a great opportunity to be of influence and be a witness for Christ in national government in India.

"But Ro," Mawii protested, "you already have the most important job in the entire world— serving the Lord Jesus. Here we are, making all these plans to reach Imphal with the gospel, and you want to go off politicking!"

She turned from him and ran from the office to their home nearby. Upstairs in her bedroom, she knelt and prayed through her tears. "Lord, help me to understand. Give me peace about this. Ro seems so enthusiastic. I should be an encouragement to him."

That night Ro wrestled with the problem as well. He appreciated Mawii's feelings but knew the ultimate decision was his. He prayed throughout much of the night, asking God to show him the right path. "Lord, help me not to consider any ambitions of my own but also to be willing to follow where you lead."

Before the night was over, he felt he had his answer. This opportunity *had* to be of God; the timing was too extraordinary to have "just happened." Besides, there were others who could take his place in the mission, but to be a member of Parliament, well, that was a responsibility that he could handle with God's help.

But to help ease Mawii's concerns, he put the reasons that helped him make his decision in writing. He tiptoed upstairs and placed the letter beside her as she slept. When she awoke the next morning and read it, her tears began to flow again. "Lord, give me confidence that you are leading Ro," she prayed.

The next morning at the breakfast table, Ro uncharacteristically discussed the decision with the children, letting them provide input. In turn, the youngsters listened attentively. Mawii was not able to concentrate as they did. For some reason, she could not stop her tears.

Ro went over to his wife and placed his arms around her reassuringly. "Sweetheart, just think what an opportunity this will be to show the rest of India what Christianity has done for our tribe. Certainly this will hold back the rising flood of resentment against missionaries. Don't you want to go back home again?"

"Oh, Ro. That's not it! You know how much I'd love to live in India again. It's just that I don't want us to do anything to displease the Lord."

"I will pray that he will give you peace about this decision, as he has given me."

His election was guaranteed. All he had to do was go to India and be there to file his candidacy before the deadline. He planned his schedule just to make sure nothing would keep him from making the filing deadline. His plane would arrive two full days before the deadline.

Ro left early, with a brief visit to Moscow for a few days included en route. All went well until his airplane left Moscow for Tashkent, on the southern tip of Russia. The pilot first announced that they would be on the ground for twenty-five minutes; then he said the time would be extended for repairs. The passengers were instructed to leave the plane and go to a hotel. Ro, along with the other passengers, went to the hotel, where they were told the delay would be even longer.

Next came word that the plane would be grounded overnight. Ro was growing increasingly concerned, but it wouldn't matter as long as the plane left early enough the next day. Finally the airport officials announced that the aircraft would be leaving. But it did not take off until the *next afternoon.*

The plane landed in Kabul, Afghanistan, and the pilot announced, "We will be staying overnight." A second overnight stay would crowd the already tight schedule, so Ro decided to change to an Afghan Airlines flight that left earlier.

The Afghan plane took off and made a scheduled stop in Lahore, Pakistan. As the plane landed, Ro saw an Indian Airlines jetliner that had been hijacked by Pakistanis going up in flames on the end of the runway.

Ro pulled out his camera and snapped several pictures when a Pakistani military man placed his hand over the lens and ordered Ro to take the film out of the camera.

The soldier barked, "What nationality are you?"

Ro replied, "I am Indian."

War was imminent between India and Pakistan over the situation in Bengladesh, so the soldiers took no chances. All the passengers were ordered off the plane. The Pakistani police then searched the aircraft and questioned the passengers, delaying the flight for six hours.

Finally, the passengers were allowed back on board the plane, and it was allowed to take off. Throughout the remainder of the flight, Ro nervously looked at his watch. It would be close.

At long last, the plane touched down in New Delhi, but it had arrived *two hours past the filing deadline.*

Khuma and several Hmar leaders had gotten word of the flight delays and were still waiting at the airport. Khuma had even checked to see if the deadline could be extended, due to the circumstances beyond their control. But he was as crushed as Ro to learn that nothing could be done.

Ro and Khuma climbed into a taxi and went to a hotel in New Delhi. Exhausted, they tried to pray for understanding before finally giving in to sleep.

Ro was too disconsolate to even talk about it. He composed a cable and sent it to Mawii. It arrived the next day at the mission office in Wheaton. When she read it, her feelings were not ones of relief but of concern for her husband. "How disappointed he must be," she said and went home to pray for him.

Back in Delhi, Ro said to Khuma, "The Lord must have a purpose in this."

With this thought in mind, the next morning he and Khuma left for Imphal, where Hmar church leaders had been planning a major evangelism crusade.

The greater Imphal metropolitan area of half a million (mostly Meitei) people did not have a single Christian church, nor had any foreigner even been permitted to preach there.

Five hundred Hmar lay workers had volunteered to serve on the evangelism teams. But since there were buses for only 320 people, those under the age of fifteen and over fifty were urged to stay behind in Sielmat and pray for the meetings. The 320 workers took along 150,000 copies of Scripture portions in the Meitei language, the most widely spoken dialect in Imphal, and in three hours had given them all away.

At the Imphal crusade Ro's brother Ramlien brought a Muslim teacher to Ro's room and introduced him. "This is Mr. Mohammed. He wishes to debate you," Ramlien explained.

Ro looked at his watch. "But I'm afraid we do not have the time." Then he noticed the man's agitated look and said, "Very well. Let's do it the way they do in the United States. You take eight minutes and tell me all that Muhammad, your prophet, has done for you for which you are excited and bubble over. Then I'll take eight minutes to tell you what Jesus has done for me for which I'm excited and bubble over. Then it will be time for me to leave. I must go speak."

The man in the long flowing robe of a Muslim priest bowed courteously and said to Ro, "You begin."

"No, you are my guest," Ro replied. "You should go first."

"But I insist."

"Very well," Ro acquiesced. "As you know, I am a Hmar tribal man. My grandfather was a headhunter, and my father was trained to be a headhunter. But God changed my father from being a savage headhunter to being a loving hearthunter for Jesus Christ. It was because of the power of God.

"I, too, have received this experience of having Christ in my heart," Ro continued. "Since I have become a Christian, I have been so sure of God's leadership that I never have to worry about what is done to me today or tomorrow. I know I have a home in heaven."

Then Ro related to him the experience of arriving back too late to file for the candidacy and how he knew that God must have an even better plan for his life.

"Jesus Christ has met every need of my life. There have been many times when I had a desperate need for money for my own living expenses when I was in school. He supplied all my needs, not once but over and over.

"There were times when I was in danger of losing my life—as a boy in the jungle, and later as a man when rebels tried to kill me. But when I turned my needs over to Jesus Christ, he met every one of them.

"The most exciting thing about life is that when you know the source of joy and peace, when you know light and life, and when you have Jesus, you have everything. That is what I have."

Ro looked at his watch. "Now, it is your turn. The Muslim shuffled uneasily, looking first at Ro then at the floor. "It's your turn," Ro repeated politely.

"No . . . ," the man said slowly and almost in a whisper. "I have nothing like that to tell you. Muhammad has not done anything like that for me. I surrender my time to you. Will you take my eight minutes and tell how Jesus can help *me?*"

Ro needed no urging. In eight minutes he told him of God's love and how Jesus had come to earth to die and redeem men from their sins and give them eternal life.

Then the Muslim priest asked, "How may I have Jesus in my heart?" They knelt together and prayed. Then Ro left in order to preach at the meeting, leaving Ramlien to talk with him.

A little later, as Ro was walking to the rostrum to speak, he noticed Ramlien and Mohammed, the Muslim priest, coming into the auditorium. He called on the Muslim and said politely, "Sir, would you come and tell everyone what happened this morning?"

The robed spiritual leader stepped to the front, looked around, and declared loudly, "I went to debate Mr. Pudaite, but instead I received Jesus Christ as my Savior."

His testimony had a remarkable effect on the listeners. Many casual observers now gave full attention to Ro's clear evangelistic message that followed.

After the crusade the converts were invited to a thirty-day course on basic Bible doctrines taught in Sielmat.

Many of the new believers came at the price of persecution, and others were rejected by their families. One of the keenest from among the new converts was the Muslim priest, whom Ro and Ramlien had led to Christ. As it turned out, he was a Muslim scholar, trained in Persian, Arabic, English, and Hebrew. Now he shared with them that he wanted to become a Christian minister.

"I have learned a great lesson," Ro later told Khuma. "I've learned that when an influential leader becomes a Christian, he is not persecuted as others are. In fact, he usually wins converts more readily. If for no other reason than this, the Lord has had a definite purpose in my coming back to India, even if I missed that political opportunity."

Ro flew back to Wheaton with a fresh ambition to seek the plan God had for him that was even greater.

# Chapter Fourteen
## *Bibles For The World!*

Ro was a man whose ambitions burned to accomplish great things for God. Yet with one door closing in India, he wondered what those things would be. He was acutely aware of the need in the world. After two millennia an estimated half of the world's population still had not even heard the name of Jesus—and some 500 million of these were in India.

He did some research and determined that it would take an incredible team of four thousand missionaries *a thousand years* to speak just *once* to everyone in India about Christ—provided that the population did not continue to grow. (Then India's population rate was *one million a month.* Today, the population is exploding at double that rate—*two million a month!* )

The solution had to lie with reaching the influential national leadership: teachers, doctors, lawyers, government leaders. But these were the very people who were least likely to be reached with conventional mission strategies.

The conversion of the Muslim priest in Imphal had made a dramatic impact on others, and Ro could see such influence being of great importance to the cause of Christ. But how to reach these important, educated, and influential leaders?

This burden lingered into summer. Ro spent hours on his knees, asking God to reveal some new method—a means of reaching India's leaders, a task that the Western churches and missionaries had failed to do.

In September his prayers were interrupted one day by a telephone company jingle "Let your fingers do the walking." It repeated itself over and over in his mind. Frustrated, Ro stopped praying.

As he rose from his knees and looked up, his eyes focused on two telephone directories on his desk. Suddenly the vision was clear. Those books listed the names and addresses of everyone in Calcutta and New Delhi who could afford a telephone. These were the best educated, most influential people—the very leaders he wanted to reach.

*That's it,* he thought. *We'll* mail *the gospel!* Ro recalled, "There are over a million telephone subscribers in India, and 98 percent of them know English. We can mail the New Testament in modern English and reach those people who are otherwise unreachable. And a Bible coming from another Indian might make it less likely to be rejected as foreign propaganda. The Bible is God's message of love and redemption. No one should die before reading it."

He reflected further and shared the idea with Mawii, who caught the vision immediately. The project became even more exciting. "By letting our 'fingers do the walking,' we can reach the whole world! The Word of God in the language of the people has always been the best missionary.

"And we can use a paperback book to help keep the costs down. But we'll have an attractive, artistic, four-color cover to get their attention."

Bibles for the whole world? The concept was staggering, to say the least. Ro said to Mawii,

"Will the board think I am crazy?" Then he answered his own question. "Maybe they will think I am crazy, but if the vision is from God, he will prepare the way."

Ro did more research and discovered that since the invention of the printing press in 1450, nearly 3 billion Bibles had been printed. However, 85 percent of these were printed in English, but *only 9 percent of the world's 5 billion people were English-speaking people.* (Today, there are 6 billion people alive on earth.)

Over *90 percent of the world's people* must share the remaining 15 percent of the world's Bibles not printed in English. The result was that *more than half of the world's people had neither seen nor read the Bible.* For example, in Iraq *fewer than three hundred thousand* Bibles have been printed *in the past two thousand years.* This amounts to one for every 140 people.

In the U.S. and Canada nearly everyone owned several copies of the Bible. It was difficult for people living in North America to imagine such a spiritual famine for God's Word in the rest of the world.

In India there was one Bible for every 320 Hindi-speaking people. In West Bengal, William Carey, father of modern missions, translated the Bible some two hundred years ago. Since then, *fewer than four hundred thousand Bibles and New Testaments had been printed in the Bengali language during these two centuries.* Yet there were *120 million* Bengalis living in India and *130 million* living in Bangladesh. That means that all of the Bengali Bibles ever printed resulted in one for every 625 people.

In the former Soviet Union, China, Africa, and much of Latin America, the figures were nearly the same, proving Ro's earlier discovery that more than half the people in the world have never seen or read a Bible.

Ro also discovered that the history of civilization bore out that in any nation where the Bible was freely circulated and available, where its precepts were understood and practiced, the people were able to take care of their own needs of food, medical attention, clothing, and shelter. Education was all but universal.

*But how can this happen unless someone gives those people living in other nations a Bible?* Ro asked. As he reflected, he realized that God had given him a simple idea (which later became his slogan)—a plan to "let the whole world read God's Word" in our generation.

At that time, there were some one billion telephone subscribers, and their names and addresses were in the phone books. Ro found that in most countries of the world, only the well-to-do, influential leaders could afford phones. So by using the phone books as a mailing list, he believed that he could reach the people who were most likely to effect change and get things done.

Ro accepted as his commission from God to find a way to publish, print, and mail a free copy of the New Testament in the language of the people to all the telephone owners. In so doing he believed it would be a part of fulfilling the prophecy of our Lord: "The gospel must first be published among all nations" (Mark 13:10).

Mawii had been working on the current issue of their newsletter, but as she listened to her husband share his vision, her eyes were wide with excitement and in sharing the joy of his plan.

A few days later Ro's neighbor, Dr. Kenneth Taylor, the man who had recently done *The Living Bible* paraphrase, called. "Ro, we're printing some *Living New Testaments* for Asian distribution. I'd like your opinion on what the artists have done for a cover picture," he said.

Ro was flattered. It was not often that an American asked his opinion on something. "I'll be right over," he said.

"Oh no," Dr. Taylor said with a chuckle. "I'm the one asking a favor. I'll come to your office." A little while later, the tall, slender Bible scholar arrived and handed Ro a paperback mock-up of the New Testament. The cover bore the title *The Greatest Is Love* and pictured a white man carrying a black child on his shoulders.

Ro swallowed hard. To him it was an obvious "red flag," a colonialist symbol that had turned off his people for generations. He looked up at his friend. "Do you really want my opinion, Ken?"

"Yes. Your frank appraisal. That's why I asked.

"Then I think you should scrap it. It's a put-down. To Americans, this is a picture of racial harmony and cooperation. But Asians know that white Americans really don't go around carrying blacks on their backs."

Dr. Taylor took the advice graciously, then asked, "What do you suggest that we use?"

Ro thought for a moment, then replied, "Give me a few minutes to think about it."

The two men walked from Ro's office to the kitchen, where he asked Mawii to pour some coffee for their guest and chat with him for a few minutes. After Dr. Taylor had finished his coffee, he returned to Ro's office to find him beaming.

"The Taj Mahal, Ken," Ro suggested. "The Taj is an Asian symbol of love, and it has that same meaning all over the world."

Dr. Taylor instantly saw the wisdom of Ro's idea. "Great! Do you have a color print or slide that we can use?"

Ro smiled and nodded. "Mawii and I visited the Taj on our last trip to India, and she took some beautiful slides. I'm sure we can find one you can use."

A few weeks later Dr. Taylor returned to Ro's office with another artist's mock-up of the new cover.

"It's beautiful!" Ro enthused. Then he added, "You know, the Lord has given me a vision of making New Testaments available to the people of India through the mail. Could we use this same edition for our project?"

"Certainly. After all, you provided the idea for the cover."

"I mean, would we have to pay royalties if we used *The Living New Testament* as the one we plan to give away?"

"For paperbacks? To be given away? No, you wouldn't need to pay," Dr. Taylor said.

With no royalties to pay, Ro figured they could do all the preparation of address labels and wrappers, including the ten-cent-postage, and still mail the New Testaments for about a dollar each. *Only* a dollar. All the mission had to do was raise a dollar to send a copy to every telephone subscriber in India, plus a dollar for every new telephone subscriber added to new directories before the mailing was completed.

Ro's board was overwhelmed by the magnitude of his vision. This exciting project with its *one-million-dollar* budget completely dwarfed the current $250,000 yearly income of the mission.

Reluctantly, his board approved an initial test printing order of fifty thousand copies for India. But Ro was more than ready to begin. An appeal was made to local church groups for volunteers to come in and type address labels, starting with the Calcutta directory.

Ro started talking up the project. At a local Christian Businessmen's Committee meeting of thirty to forty men, he held up one of the promotional copies and said, "If you'll buy one like this for ten dollars, I'll send nine more to India." Ro "sold" over thirty copies on that basis at the one meeting.

His exhilaration over the response to his plan was suddenly dampened by a call from the printer. He would need ten thousand dollars by the next week in order to secure the order and buy the paper for printing. "Since we're doing the job at cost," he told Ro, "we can't afford to put up the money for the paper ourselves."

After he hung up the phone, Ro turned to God. "Lord," he prayed, "if we get ten thousand dollars by next week, we will surely know that you are behind our Bible mailing. I can never raise that much money in such a short time."

On Sunday morning Ro shared his burden with the congregation where he was speaking. They had five minutes of silent prayer for Ro and the project.

After the service Ro went to the home of a church elder for dinner. A young couple came by to ask for him. Ro met with them and listened to their story.

"Recently," the husband began, "we sold our old home and bought a new one. As it turned out, we paid less for the new house, and we've been praying about what to do with the difference. We both agree that you should have this check for fifteen hundred dollars for your Bibles."

Ro was overwhelmed at the gift. He was still quite buoyant when he went to the church for the evening service. As he crossed the church parking lot, he saw an elderly woman standing with a large brown grocery bag. Thinking she might need help climbing the stairs into the church, he offered, "Can I help you?"

"I want to help *you*," she replied. "I have something to give you for your Bibles." And she gave him the paper bag. Looking inside, Ro saw that the bag was stuffed with loose currency— ones and fives mostly. When he counted it later, it came to over a thousand dollars, which the woman had saved by putting aside "small" bills for the Lord's work.

At the time for the evening service, the church elders were not yet in the sanctuary. They had been meeting before the service and finally a spokesman came to the front of the church. Calling Ro to the pulpit, he gave him a check for funds the church had in been holding in reserve for a special mission project. It was more than half of what Ro needed.

There were other unexpected gifts that came in and by the end of the week the miracle had occurred. The money—all of the ten thousand dollars that Ro needed—had come in.

It proved to be the way that God would bless those initial efforts to finance the Bible mailing. Miracle after miracle happened, and Ro and Mawii knew without a doubt that this was God's doing.

Fueled by Ro's efforts and other promotions, contributions continued to arrive and began to give credibility to the concept of Bibles For The World, the new name given to Partnership Mission by its Board of Directors. The ministry received coins from youngsters' piggy banks, collections from Vacation Bible School projects, dollars from teenage baby-sitters and old-age pensioners.

Along with the money came scores of local volunteers to help address, wrap, and mail the Bibles. In Ro's edition featuring the Taj Mahal, they included a brief introduction written by Ro, giving his own testimony and asking the reader to write him with any questions he or she might have concerning Jesus Christ.

An office was opened in New Delhi to receive any mail in response to that invitation, and letters began to pour in. From the initial test mailing of fifty thousand copies, Ro received over twenty-two thousand responses. Some excerpts:

This is my first experience in reading the Bible. . . . I am a Hindu.

Thank you for the holy Book. Please send me other literature. My friend is also interested.

I read . . . and I feel fully influenced with what the Bible says. I have no words to say . . . but I think I have reached a height where I see nothing but Christ who died so that we might live. No one on earth can shake my love for Christ. I want to know more about him, about the Bible, and about myself.

I have come to know that you have a Bible in modern English. If it is so, kindly let me know. . . . I am a Muslim.

The abundant requests for additional New Testaments had not been anticipated but the board decided to send them as well--so long as the funds held out.

The Tyndale Foundation of Dr. Ken Taylor then made an unprecedented offer: We will match every dollar that your mission raises, in units of $50,000, up to $250,000.

Ro was stunned, but confident that these higher goals could be achieved. He demonstrated his thoughts to his board with a rubber band. "You can stretch this rubber band only so far before it breaks. But when you stretch your faith, the farther you stretch it, the stronger it becomes."

Response letters were now coming by the thousands from Indians eager to share their new-found faith with Ro. Many of them also requested more information about Jesus Christ:

I am very grateful to you for sending me this sacred Bible. I was looking for someone who could guide me to such a path of brightness. I am a Sikh boy of age 23.

Thank you very much for this book, *The Greatest Is Love*. . . . This is a precious book, now I daily read it and do rejoice. I want to know more about your Christ and his people.

The other day I saw in my friend's house *The Greatest Is Love*. What a fine book you have produced. I would also like to possess it if it is of no inconvenience to you.

Only one letter from among the many hundreds that arrived each week was not appreciated. A secretary at the New Delhi office that Ro had set up to handle the huge volume of mail was suspicious of a parcel addressed to Ro. It was soon discovered that the package was a letter bomb. Fortunately, it didn't go off and was taken away by the authorities to be destroyed.

They passed the 300,000 mark after sending that many New Testaments to India. With 900,000 copies to go, Ro began looking beyond India. In their monthly newsletter and mailings, he listed other Asian countries with manageable telephone subscriber numbers: Nepal, 6,200; Burma (now Myanmar), 162,000; Thailand, 152,000; Ceylon (now Sri Lanka), 62,000; Sikkim, 250, and so on.

Ro hoped that churches and individuals might help him match these various countries and cities with sponsors in the United States.

The Reverend Lud Golz, a pastor in Novelty, Ohio, asked his children if they'd like to take little

Sikkim with its scant 250 telephone subscribers as their Christmas gift for Jesus. The Golz family eagerly agreed and looked up the country in their encyclopedia: population 200,000; Buddhist and Hindu religions; no Christian churches.

The Golz family prayed and sacrificed some of their Christmas presents in order to send Bibles to the leaders of Sikkim. Mom and Dad supervised and typed the address labels, while the four kids helped pack the New Testaments and apply the postage stamps. Even five-year-old Jess could do that.

Providentially, the New Testaments were mailed just as that country was being hit by an attempted revolution and coup, with news reports coming of violent fighting in the streets.

The Golz family prayed for the people and for those in Sikkim who would be receiving the Bibles. The first of many response letters came just a few weeks later:

> My friend and I returned home
> from fighting and found a package
> on the doorstep. It was the Bible you
> sent. We read it with great interest.
> The next day we did not demonstrate
> against the government.

Ro later learned that the writer of that letter was the leader of the revolutionary movement. Hope Cooke, a beautiful American woman who had married King Chokyal of Sikkim, had escaped from the country and possible death only because the revolutionary leader did not demonstrate on the day she sought to escape.

When it became evident to Ro and Mawii that they were going to complete the mailing to India by year-end, they decided to see firsthand just how and why the New Testaments were being so well received. They booked a flight back to their homeland.

When they landed in New Delhi, the press was quite curious about the thousands of colorful New Testaments being mailed into India from an overseas Indian. At the suggestion of his friend, V. V. Purie, Ro called a news conference, thinking this was the best and fastest way to get the word about their project to the news media.

A great number of reporters came, representing the *India Express, Times of India, Hindustan Times,* and other leading newspapers. At the news conference, reporters asked Ro pointed questions, and the journalists listened courteously to his answers.

A reporter from the *Hindustan Times* stood and asked, "Do I hear you correctly, that it is your intention to mail a copy of the Bible to every telephone subscriber in the world? If so, when are you going to mail Bibles to Russia?"

Ro's answer was direct but diplomatic. "We do not want to smuggle Bibles, although we do not condemn those who do. Our policy will be to take them through the 'front door.' Right now the Russian government prohibits the distribution of Bibles in the Soviet Union. My answer to you is, as soon as the door is open, we will mail Bibles to Russia."

A reporter from the *Times of India* stood and said, "Have you not read about the Cultural Exchange Program of August 9, 1971? That agreement between India and Russia includes cultural book exchanges between the two nations. Under this program Russia has shipped more than 2 million volumes of communist literature into India, but India has not responded. Since the Bible is your cultural book, you should go to the Soviet embassy and ask permission to mail your cultural book into Russia. And if they say no, will you call another news conference because we would all like to know that!"

Not two hours later Ro had called the Soviet embassy for an appointment.

The next day the articles came out. To Ro's amazement every one of them was friendly. For him, it was an exciting contrast to a flurry of negative publicity over the recent expulsion of a missionary.

But even more exciting for Ro was the appointment he had with the cultural attaché at the Russian embassy. When the official called Ro into his office, the Russian already knew what their discussion would cover. The attaché came to greet Ro. *"Russi-Hindi, bhai, bhai!"* he said with a wide smile and open arms. Ro understood his Hindi greeting which meant, "Russians and Indians are brothers!"

Ro returned the greeting, *"Hindi-Russi, bhai, bhai!"* ("Indians and Russians are brothers!")

He learned that two Russian *Tass Agency* "journalists," probably KGB agents, had been at his news conference the day before. They had no doubt given the full account of the reporters' comments.

The Russians were not about to give the India press a major incident for the Western press to trumpet around the globe. But they had already decided to give in and let this man mail Bibles to Russia from India.

"I know all about your plan to send Bibles," the attaché told him frankly. "We will permit it with certain conditions."

"What are they?" asked Ro.

"First, you must use the 1956 edition of the Russian Bible. It is published by the Publication Division of the USSR and has the government imprimatur so that no one will question it."

Ro nodded. Inwardly he was glad. They might have wanted him to use a hard-to-read, archaic translation. But it turned out that this was a modern translation, approved by most evangelical leaders.

"The second condition is that you must print and mail the Bibles only from India. And third, you must not use this exchange program as a publicity stunt or for your own propaganda purposes in the West."

When Ro left the Russian embassy, he had their full approval and the conditions were totally acceptable to him. His heart soared as he considered the miracle that had just taken place.

Ro's search for a copy of the scarce Russian Bible proved to be a greater problem. He tried all of his contacts to little avail. Finally, his close friend and Bible printer, V. V. Purie, who knew of the need, called his brother in London, who traveled to Moscow on a two-day business trip. While there, he located two copies of the Bible and on his return to London mailed a copy to Ro and sent the other copy to New Delhi to use in making the films for the printing plates.

Then came an even greater problem. Ro couldn't locate any "official" Russian telephone directories. He learned that the Russians, ever so paranoid about state secrets, did not publish addresses in their telephone books. Only the names and telephone numbers were included.

But he also learned that there were "official" directories, mainly for the Communist Party faithful, that did indeed contain all of the needed information.

Once again V. V. Purie came to the rescue. He suggested, "Let's have lunch with Mr. M. L. Bardhwaj. He's the former principal private secretary to Prime Minister Nehru. Perhaps he can help."

Over lunch Purie said to their guest, "Tell me, how long has it been since you have last visited with your old friend, Leonid Brezhnev?" (Before he became the communist Chairman and ruler of the USSR, Brezhnev was an aide to Nikita Khrushchev, then the chief communist dictator.)

"I have not seen Leonid in a long, long time," Bardhwaj replied. "It has been many years since we worked together. I am retired now and do not have money to travel outside of India."

Purie said, "Look, it's not good for friends not to see one another. When do you want to go to Moscow? I will pay for your expenses."

Bardhwaj smiled. "What's the catch?"

"Nothing much," Purie answered. "Really. I just want you to bring back telephone books for Russian cities that have addresses as well as names and telephone numbers."

"That's all? I can do that!"

In two weeks, Bardhwaj was in Moscow. On the night before he left Moscow to return to New Delhi, the Russian leader had a farewell dinner in honor of his friend Bardhwaj. Brezhnev then asked, "Is there anything I can do to make your trip more memorable? Anything at all, my dear friend?"

Bardhwaj looked up and said, "Yes. There is one thing." And he asked Brezhnev for the phone books with names and addresses. The next day uniformed couriers came to his hotel with four huge hardbound copies of the priceless directories. Bardhwaj brought them back to India with him and gave them to V. V. Purie.

Soon the printing presses were rolling at Thomson Press in New Delhi, each day producing thousands of Russian Bibles.

Students in the Department of Russian Studies at Jawaralal Nehru University wrote out names and addresses on labels using photocopies of the scarce Russian phone books. Before long, Ro was mailing then thousand Russian Bibles a month of the into the Soviet Union from his homeland of India.

Sensing a great interest in New Delhi in their Bible mailing to India, Ro decided to try an experiment. He rented a 650-seat auditorium called the Sapru House and placed ads in the capital's two leading newspapers. The ads were announcements inviting those who had received *The Greatest Is Love (The Living New Testament)* to come the next evening at 7:00 p.m. and "hear the life story of the man who sent you this book."

"I wonder if there will be any response," Ro mused to Mawii as he paced up and down in their hotel room. "What if no one comes? This should have been planned well in advance. Why didn't I think of it sooner?"

An hour and a half before the meeting was to begin, the auditorium manager phoned Ro.

"The building is already packed! We're turning people away. Please come right away. We don't know what to do with all these people!"

Ro and Mawii hurried over, and Ro quickly took charge. First he introduced Mawii who gave a brief testimony. Then he spoke for forty-five minutes, telling what the Lord had done for him and his tribe. He concluded by saying, "If there are those who want to talk to us further about believing in Jesus Christ, will you please come to the front? We will try to help you." About half the audience tried to crowd forward!

Ro and Mawii tried to talk to as many inquirers as possible, but soon Ro was hoarse, and there was still a crowd of people who hadn't heard. So Ro went back to the podium. "My friends," he told them, "there are still many waiting to hear about Jesus Christ. It is not possible to see you all tonight. Could you please call my office tomorrow instead? We will be there to help you. May God be with you." And the crowd was dismissed.

The next day the office telephone rang continuously. Ro and Mawii were ecstatic as they shared Christ with the many inquirers.

"Surely this is all the evidence we need that God is behind this idea," Ro said. "He is blessing and using his Word in a greater way than I ever dreamed possible."

On a trip to Imphal sometime later, Ro noticed a well-dressed, dignified gentleman reading a copy of *The Greatest Is Love*. Ro sat beside him and asked him about what he was reading. The man wondered how Ro knew so much about the book.

"Look inside the front cover," Ro told him. The man turned the pages to the introduction, with Ro's picture and comments.

The man laughed. "You rascal--it's you!" Then he asked Ro questions about what he was reading. Before the plane landed, Ro had introduced him to Jesus Christ. Ro followed up that meeting with others. The man, as it turned out, was Chief Justice of the Supreme Court of India and earlier served as India's ambassador to Washington, D.C.

Following the meeting at the New Delhi auditorium, Mawii observed, "Ro, the whole atmosphere seems so charged with the power of God, and witnessing seems just as natural as breathing." Later they were heading for another meeting with more opportunities to share Christ. At Imphal, when they got off the plane, the first to greet them was Chawnga. As Ro embraced his father in greeting, Chawnga asked, "How is it coming, my son? Tell me about the Bible distribution."

"Well, my father," Ro answered, "God has done great things, and we will soon see the completion of India."

"*All* of India?" Chawnga exclaimed, truly amazed.

"Yes. We will have sent a copy to over one million telephone subscribers--1.2 million to be exact. But even more important is what God is doing with the Books." Ro told his father of the meeting in New Delhi. "I have never seen so much hunger for the Bible and never expected to see so much spiritual enthusiasm for Christianity in India, especially in New Delhi!"

Chawnga shook his head in wonder. "In New Delhi? I didn't think that Hindus would be interested at all."

"Nor did I. But that's what's so exciting! It *works!* It's the power of God's Word speaking directly to the reader. The Holy Spirit helps them understand what it says to them. It really works, my father," Ro said excitedly.

"Bible distribution is the key to reaching our world for Christ. We can tell them about Jesus in their own language and reach the entire world through the Word. I'm convinced of it!"

Tears welled up in the older man's eyes. "My son, God has truly opened to you a great horizon—a plan for all of us to go to heaven alive."

Ro asked, "What do you mean?"

The elder Pudaite replied confidently, "Don't you remember the words of Mark—'the gospel must first be published among all nations.' And Matthew said, 'And this gospel of the kingdom shall be preached in all the world for a witness; and then shall the end come.' You must continue to mail Bibles in order to get the job done soon."

# Chapter Fifteen
## *Beyond the Horizon*

Bibles For The World was now the name of the mission. BFW began as a pilot program for Partnership Ministries, the name for the work of the Indo-Burma Pioneer Mission started by Ro and Mawii at the urgent request of Watkin Roberts. Now that the new effort of Bible distribution was the major thrust of the mission it was logical to change its name.

The flames that were fanned by Roberts's obedience to God's call in 1910 had spread out all across northeast India. One of his first Hmar converts prayed that his son might one day grow up, receive an education, and translate the Bible into their tribal language.

God answered those sincere prayers but in so doing went far beyond that initial vision. He gave Rochunga Pudaite an even greater mission—and Bibles For The World marches on.

After one million copies were mailed to India, New Testaments were mailed to Nepal, Bhutan, Sri Lanka, Afghanistan, Bangladesh, Pakistan, and Singapore. Providentially, Bibles were mailed to Afghanistan just at the time of their war with Russia.

During the Cold War, more than 750,000 Russian New Testaments were sent to Moscow, Kiev and other cities in the former Soviet Union from India. Ro used the Russia-India Cultural Exchange Program to advantage and ensured that the Bibles would get through.

There is no way to know whether so many copies of God's Word sent to Russia's leaders contributed to the breakup of the Soviet Union, but response letters from a great many Soviet citizens who found Christ through the reading of the Russian New Testament show that the Bibles had a dramatic impact on individual lives.

The same thing happened in other nations that were ruled by communist, military, or religious dictatorships where Bibles were able to get through.

(By 1998, Bibles For The World had sent over 14 million copies of God's Word into more than one hundred different countries.)

\*     \*     \*

On January 17, 1975, a distinguished visitor pulled into the driveway of the Pudaite home in Wheaton. Mr. T. N. Kaul, India's ambassador to the United States, had come for an important visit.

Ro and Mawii welcomed him, having met him on several occasions and visited his office in Washington, D.C.

Mr. Kaul had been inducted into foreign service by the late Prime Minister Nehru, and he was one of India's most respected civil servants. He'd served as India's ambassador in London, Moscow, and Peking (now Beijing) and was India's foreign secretary before his assignment to Washington.

Mr. Kaul exchanged pleasantries with Ro but quickly indicated that his presence in Wheaton was an official visit, and he got down to business.

Ambassador Kaul said, "You probably know by now that two days ago the Mizo underground murdered Mr. Aria, inspector general of the police, as well as several of his officers in a raid in Aijal."

Ro nodded soberly. For ten years there had been unrest and violence in Mizoram after the 1966-67 *mautam* (famine). Mizoram, then only a district in northeast India without the influence and power of a state, endured great suffering as a result of the famine. Unknown to the outside world, many people had died of starvation, a fact that a number of state and national leaders tried to keep quiet.

The government in Assam ignored the appeals of the young Mizo leader, Laldenga, who simply sought to help his people. He organized the Mizo Famine Front, and when he could not get assistance from the state or regional governments, nor from New Delhi, Laldenga looked to leaders in neighboring East Pakistan (now Bangladesh) for help.

With the help of East Pakistan, which supplied arms, Laldenga's organization, renamed the Mizo National Front, declared independence from India.

The Mizo National Front withdrew its participation in Indian political affairs and was forced underground by India's military actions, which erupted immediately after their declaration of independence. Next, the city of Aijal was bombed by the Indian air force, and a full scale war was waged between the Indian army and the Mizo National Front.

Laldenga set up the MNF "capital" and headquarters near Chittagong as guerrilla warfare broke out all throughout the state.

Warfare continued for almost a decade. When Bangladesh gained its independence from Pakistan in 1971, Laldenga looked to China and North Vietnam for its arms and guerrilla training.

The guerrilla war gained in intensity as young recruits returned from their training in China and took up arms. Many were caught by the army and imprisoned. Other men and women, suspected of MNF ties, were also put in prison or military custody.

As is the case in guerrilla warfare, many innocent people, including youngsters, were killed or wounded in bomb attacks, sabotage, and violence. No one was safe. Each person was suspicious of everyone else. People lived in constant fear of both the army and the MNF guerrillas. They were caught in the middle of an intense war.

By now, the Indian army had destroyed most of the outlying villages and brought the people into what they called "grouping centres," which were heavily guarded camps.

Ironically, Mizoram claimed to have the highest concentration of Christians among its population (95 percent in a state of seven hundred thousand people). But the people were afraid, and the Mizo church bells were silent. As if that weren't enough, Christians were not allowed to assemble for worship services or for other church events.

It was this situation that Ambassador Kaul referred to in his conversation with Ro. The assassination two days earlier of the inspector general of police and his officers was merely the latest in a series of terrible killings.

"Reverend," Ambassador Kaul explained, "if the war continues as it has, Mrs. Gandhi [then the prime minister] will be forced to take even stronger actions against the Mizo people."

Ro winced. Mawii, although a Hmar, had been born in Mizoram. He knew many Hmars who lived there. In fact, H. K. Bawichhuaka, the son of the best friend of Watkin Roberts, whom Ro had visited in prison prior to India's independence, had become one of the top Mizo leaders. Ironically, Bawichhuaka had been a patriotic Freedom Fighter for India's independence struggle with Great Britain. Now he was still for India, but he opposed both the Mizo National Front and Indian army for their unrestrained use of war and violence to accomplish their aims.

The ambassador continued his appeal to Ro. "Mrs. Gandhi loves the Mizo hill people as her father did before her. But the prime minister is forced to act.

"The Home Ministry has already sanctioned several troop divisions to be deployed to northeast India. If that plan is carried out in Mizoram and the Indian army invades, that region will never be the same.

"I am asking you, on behalf of Prime Minister Gandhi, to consider going to Mizoram to find a formula for peace. You know the people, you know the language. What do you say, my friend?"

For a moment Ro said nothing. He just let it all sink in. Finally he said, "I will pray about it, and you will have my answer within two weeks."

For the next thirteen days, Ro barely slept. His time was spent thinking, praying, and waiting for divine guidance. He was not confident of his skills as a negotiator or peacemaker. And humanly speaking, he was afraid. If he was to succeed, he would have to make the attempt as a private citizen. If he came as an official representative of the Indian government, he could be killed as a spy.

The next day was Sunday, the deadline for informing Ambassador Kaul. After church Ro retired to the living room to pray, still uncertain as to what he should do. Mawii came into the room and announced, "Ro, one of our favorite preachers is on television. Will you come and watch?"

As Ro entered the family room, he saw that Dr. Stuart Briscoe was speaking on the Chicago Sunday Evening Club telecast of the local PBS station. Dr. Briscoe was announcing the text for his television message: Blessed are the peacemakers: for they shall be called the children of God.

The speaker had Ro's attention. Dr. Briscoe told viewers, "In our troubled world, Christians must be peacemakers. If Christians are not willing to become peacemakers, then who will?" It was as if God himself were speaking directly to Ro.

At the conclusion of the message, Ro went to his office and wrote a plan for dealing with the crisis. He listed ten criteria that he said were essential to success. These included prerequisites that Ro would go as a private citizen for peace feelers; that he'd have instant access to Prime Minister Gandhi, and that the Indian government issue "safe conduct" passes that Ro could give to anyone he sought to meet with so that the rebels could avoid capture, arrest, and imprisonment during the peace process.

All of his conditions were accepted, and he flew to New Delhi with Khuma, whose wisdom and judgment he trusted. They met with Indira Gandhi for briefing and procedures. From there they flew to Aijal, the official capital of Mizoram (which had been only a district but in recent years had become a Union Territory, with a lieutenant governor and chief minister).

Ro met with the governor, S. K. Chhibber, first and told him of his mission. Then he met with the chief minister, Mr. Chhunga, who was so desperate for peace that he offered to step down in favor of Laldenga if the rebel leader came back because of peace.

He also met with several Mizo leaders, who knew and trusted him. He asked them to get the word to the rebels that he wanted to discuss peace prospects with them. They reminded Ro that a meeting with rebel leaders could be dangerous—that his life would be in danger from both sides.

On one occasion when Ro was in Aijal, Mizo revolutionary leaders announced they were going to set off bombs in five separate places. Ro heard an airplane swoop low over the city. But instead of bombs, it dropped a flurry of propaganda leaflets that littered the city. Ro went outside to pick up several of the leaflets and then went back inside to his room.

Ro had just settled into a chair to read from a book when someone burst into his room. The man flew across the room in an instant and jammed a pistol against Ro's chest.

"Don't move!" he shouted.

"What do you want?" Ro asked.

"I have come to eliminate you! You are a *spy,* and you must be killed!"

"I am not a spy," Ro told him calmly.

"You are an agent of the government!"

"Young man, I am not a spy. Nor am I a government agent. I am an agent of peace who wants to see this killing stop," Ro added.

The young rebel did not seem satisfied, and his pistol was jammed further into Ro's ribs.

"Are you a Christian?" Ro asked him.

The man nodded. Ro continued.

"Since you are a Christian and I am a Christian, then will you let me pray before you do anything?"

Ro eased himself out of the chair. "I am going to kneel by this chair and pray."

The guerrilla didn't take away the gun but merely pressed it against Ro's back as he knelt by the chair. Ro uttered a quick, silent prayer, then began to pray aloud.

"Lord, I pray for this man sent here to kill me. I pray that you will keep him from harm in all of this fighting and conflict. I pray that he will not be killed. I ask you to move in the hearts of all the Christians in northeast India on both sides, that each one might be sensitive to you.

"Lord, you have told us how much you love each person. Please open the eyes of the people that they may see love and beauty in the hearts of their fellowmen. Show them love from your Word.

"Heavenly Father, I pray that you will help us find a way to live in peace and stop the killing and violence."

Before he finished his prayer, Ro felt the easing of the pressure of the pistol barrel at his back. When he finished, the man had put his gun away and was walking toward the door.

"Wait!" Ro called to him. "Now that you know who I am and my true motives, I want you to take a message to your leaders and to your people that I came here in peace and goodwill.

"Tell your people not to kill anyone or set off any bombs tomorrow. By having a cease fire on Independence Day, it will be a signal that a confidence exists between us. We can find ways to explore peace initiatives.

"But if the Mizo National Front sets off bombs or kills anyone, I'll know you have no intentions for peace. I will leave, and you will never see my face again!"

They were strong words, but the man understood. He left without saying anything.

The next day, Independence Day, came. Ro listened morning, afternoon, and night but heard no gunfire or bomb explosions. The rebels heard the message!

Governor S. K. Chhibber called him that evening and said, "Come and join me in a celebration. This is the first time since 1966 that Independence Day in the capital has not been marred by bombs and gunfire. It's a historic day!"

Eventually rebel leaders became a little more trusting of Ro and agreed to meet him regularly. Most of these meetings were held in out-of-the-way places, usually after midnight.

Ro was told not to bring a flashlight, tape recorder, or a concealed weapon. Ro sent word through two trusted messengers to have the rebel leaders meet him at his home in Manipur for peace discussions and possible solutions to the conflict.

The negotiations took him throughout all of northeast India and many times to New Delhi. Stress and fatigue were constant. One afternoon he checked into the Ashok Hotel and immediately collapsed in utter fatigue on the bed. He fell into a deep sleep and did not wake up until the next day at noon.

Ro was getting ready the next day when he got an urgent telephone call. The caller said, "Mrs. Gandhi would like for you to meet with her and spend a few minutes. Can you come?"

"Of course," Ro told him. "What time is the appointment?"

"Can you come at four o'clock?"

"Yes, I'll be there."

It was a Sunday afternoon, and the streets were less crowded as the cab made its way toward the prime minister's residence. Ro was escorted to the back of the mansion, to a beautiful lawn, where there were two chairs and a table. On the table was a blue leather-covered Bible. Ro recognized it as the one he had given to Indira Gandhi. He was puzzled by its presence on the table.

When Mrs. Gandhi came, she invited him to sit and have tea with her. After a while she said, "You gave me that Bible. Do you remember? It was when you first came."

Then she looked at Ro intently. "Tell me, if someone has problems larger than he or she can handle, can anyone find help from this book?"

Ro did not overlook the opportunity. He said, "In order for the teaching of the Bible to be meaningful and helpful to you, you must first get to know its Author."

"Who is the Author?" she asked.

"The Author is Jesus Christ. You will find his help for every need or problem," Ro replied.

Ro gave his own testimony of how the Book had helped him in incredible ways and how it had changed the entire lives and culture of the Hmar people.

"If you know the Author, he will open the Book for you," Ro told the prime minister.

Mrs. Gandhi listened carefully. "Tell me more," she said.

Ro was amazed at her openness.

He leaned toward her respectfully and told her in simple, inspired words how the Bible could tell her how to become a believer in Jesus Christ and experience God's love, forgiveness, guidance, and strength.

Their time together was unhurried and she listened respectfully. She showed a genuine interest in his words, and she leaned over toward Ro and said softly, "This is the most meaningful moment in my life." She took his hand and squeezed it warmly.

"We will talk again," she promised him.

On one of his other trips to New Delhi, Ro went to meet with the home secretary, where he discovered another matter in which he could help, but it was quite by accident. As he walked into the office of the home secretary and was ushered to a chair in front of his desk, his eyes caught a file lying on the papers on top of the desk.

The file had a handwritten notation on it: "Expulsion Order for Rev. Mark Buntain."

Ro pointed to the file. "May I read this?"

"Oh no! It's 'Top Secret,' and I can't let you read it," the home secretary told him.

"But you know that Rev. Mark Buntain is a missionary. I am also a missionary. If you expel my fellow missionary from India, I will also leave India. Immediately." Ro knew that his critical role in the Mizo peace process was important to the home secretary.

"Do you know this Buntain fellow?" he asked Ro.

"Yes. And I also know that he is doing a great work. I am aware of the complaint they have made about him. But these complaints cannot be taken seriously. Someone is jealous of him. You must not expel him."

The home secretary did not answer. Ro said, "If you will not give me a copy of that file then I will intervene with the prime minister. I will somehow get a copy of that order."

"Can you vouch for this man?"

"Yes," Ro replied. "Without question."

The home secretary persisted. "If we find out later that he is truly anti-Indian or maybe a subversive, will you be willing to bear the consequences of vouching for his character?"

"I will," Ro said emphatically.

"Then I will put this Expulsion Order on hold. But I'll have my assistant draft a letter that if this man, Rev. Mark Buntain, is discovered to be a CIA agent or is in any way working against India, we will have to hold you responsible. I am afraid that it's likely the government will treat you as a *counterspy* if something like that happens."

"I will vouch for him," Ro told him.

When the letter was brought to him to sign, Ro did so without hesitation, so Mark Buntain's expulsion order was stayed.

Later, after more meetings with the Mizo leaders in Manipur, Ro called for an Indian air force helicopter to pick up the men and ferry them to Parva, the last town in Mizoram, on the Bangladesh border. From there the rebel leaders would take a secret message to Laldenga, whose headquarters were over the border in Bangladesh.

The important message, hidden under the inner sole in the shoe of one of the men, was on its way. Ro watched as the helicopter rose into the sky and flew toward the south.

From that first communiqué from Ro to the Mizo leader, Laldenga, there were subsequent assurances of cooperation in the peace process. Soon a stream of messages and information flowed into Manipur, where Ro eventually was able to assemble his long-awaited *Formula for Peace in Mizoram.*

He finally presented it to Prime Minister Indira Gandhi--after a year and a half of efforts. She thanked him sincerely when he gave her the copies of the plan, keeping one for himself.

Mrs. Gandhi shook her head and held out her hand, "You are not supposed to keep a copy."

"But I have no other copy of the text and want to keep a file copy."

"I'm sorry, but this is a sensitive matter," she told Ro. "It has to be kept very confidential. I do not want any news leaks that might undermine our efforts. And, if circumstances prove to be unfavorable, I may have to destroy this document so no one else will know of its contents."

Reluctantly, Ro handed over his copy of the peace plan that he had written.

A few weeks after he had returned to Wheaton, he got word that hostile operations by the army and security forces in Mizoram had been suspended following an understanding between Laldenga and the Indian government toward a peace process.

Laldenga returned to negotiate for his native Mizoram within the framework of the Indian constitution. It took another ten years to accomplish everything that Ro had laid out in his *Formula for Peace in Mizoram* but it gave him great satisfaction when the final agreement was signed.

Finally the Indian government and the Mizo leader, Laldenga, sat down to sign the agreement they had reached. The entire state celebrated the peace that had come at long last. Ironically, Ro was not present at the signing or celebration.

His friend V. V. Purie, a founder (along with his son) of *India Today,* that country's largest newsmagazine (called the *Newsweek* of India) telephoned Ro in Wheaton. "Why have you not come to India for the celebration in Mizoram?" Purie asked his longtime friend.

"I was not invited," Ro said simply.

Purie was amazed. "That is cruel! They should not forget the man who initiated a way for peace in Mizoram. I know what a personal price you had to pay."

Ro had only shared with a few close friends the details of his role in the peace process. In order to avoid being labeled a spy, he had kept a totally independent position and so had not received any compensation for his services or expenses. He had had to pay five hundred thousand rupees to cover the overseas travel, meals, and lodging—as well as other expenses—to achieve the success now being celebrated.

It was painful for Ro to be ignored at this historic moment. Humanly, he was vulnerable to hurt feelings. Yet, as he talked with his friend, he was inwardly rebuked for this self-pity.

He did not linger on the slight, whether it was intended or not. He thought of his own hurt feelings only for a moment, then shared his thoughts with his friend: "V. V., it is true that I have been ignored. And I suppose I do feel hurt over that. But Jesus, my example, was not only ignored—he was persecuted and crucified. I have not suffered anything in comparison.

"Besides, as a Christian, I want to give God the glory that comes with such good things. Without him, there would still be only killing and conflict in Mizoram. It is God who has brought peace. He should get the glory."

Some time later his own feelings of hurt were assuaged and vindicated when he received a letter of appreciation from the new prime minister, Rajiv Gandhi, son of Indira who had been assassinated.

Rajiv Gandhi had apparently been going through various files, perhaps to better prepare himself for leadership of his government, when he discovered the case file on Ro's mission.

Gandhi wrote a letter to Ro, which said in part: "I just want you to know that it was [because of] the efforts of people like you that Mizoram is now celebrating peace and statehood."

Ro continued to immerse himself in the ministry of Bibles For The World. He was as busy as ever, often with more than a hundred speaking engagements every year in which he inspired audiences with the dramatic stories of his life and remarkable illustrations from tens of thousands of letters sent to him in response to the New Testaments sent out.

Several people approached Ro about doing a movie based on his life story. One man told Ro,

"I will finance it myself. I will give a million dollars to produce it!"

Ro and Mawii agreed to pray about it. Neither of them was particularly interested in their life story being turned into a film, but Ro met with close friends, who told him that such a tool could have remarkable results in telling others about Jesus and Bibles For The World. In the end it was the strong testimony aspect of the project that won over Ro and Mawii.

Ro agreed to the project, and a producer in Hollywood began to set up the shooting schedule, hired actors, set designers, and crew; and arranged for sound stages and equipment rentals.

Then a call came less than two weeks before the start of production. The man who had committed the financing was defaulting. The money was not there! He never had it in the first place.

Ro called a close friend and asked him to fly out to Hollywood and meet with the producer in order to shut down the production before any more money was spent.

The producer said that commitments had already been made and that contracts called for the actors and some others to get paid even if the production was cancelled.

So Ro's friend flew back to Wheaton with a plan to move ahead with the production in stages, as funds became available.

Ro and Mawii prayed that if God wanted the film made, he would show them by providing the funds. Miraculously, but not without serious prayer and stressful deadlines, the motion picture was produced.

*Beyond the Next Mountain,* at a cost of over $2.2 million (which God wonderfully provided) was directed by Rolf Forsberg *(Peace Child)* and James Collier *(The Hiding Place, Joni)* and has brought Ro's story to countless others in theaters, television, and videos in the U.S. and overseas.

Despite the recognition that American audiences have given to him, Ro has not forgotten his homeland. He conceived a thank-you to the churches and Christians in America who, for nearly four decades, have helped Ro with his great vision and the dreams he shared with Chawnga and Watkin Roberts.

In 1990 Ro brought the India Children's Choir to tour the U.S. and Canada. Youngsters, ages eight to twelve, made up five different choirs that toured through 1996. Each choir sang at 250 - 300 events every year and performed a total of over fifteen hundred different concert events, at churches, schools and on television during that period of time.

The India Children's Choir, headed by Mary Pudaite-Keating (Ro and Mawii's gifted daughter), has performed on *Good Morning America, The 700 Club, Hour of Power, 100 Huntley Street* and a number of other TV programs. In 1997 they sang to a potential audience of *one billion people* on India's national television network.

The performance by the India Children's Choir of *Headhunter to Hearthunter* (written and composed by Ronald K. Wells) is a powerful, dramatic, and deeply emotional presentation of what God has done in the lives of people in northeast India.

Over the past decade, Bibles For The World has addressed the matter of succession and restructuring in light of Ro's eventual retirement, addressing new Bible translation and distribution opportunities, and changes in technology.

During that process of restructuring and reorganization, the board of BFW asked John Pudaite, Ro's son, to assume the role of vice president and to take over much of the day-to-day operational details of BFW that Ro, as president, and Mawii, as executive vice president, had been responsible for. The reorganization was to free Ro and Mawii to concentrate more on speaking, writing, and ministry projects for the organization.

In 1996 the board voted to move Bibles For The World to Colorado Springs, Colorado, taking advantage of opportunities to network with other evangelical Christian organizations based there and to joint-venture some of its ministries.

In 1998 the Evangelical Free Church of India and Partnership Mission Society leaders unanimously voted to make Ro the president of the newly founded Trinity College and Seminary to be located in New Delhi.

After forty years in Wheaton, Illinois, Ro and Mawii relocated to Colorado Springs, in the shadow of Pikes Peak and the Cheyenne mountains that remind them of their beloved homeland.

"God has been so good to us," says Ro. "Some mornings I wake up and ask myself, *Can it really be true?* And it is. I can only praise God for taking me across so many different horizons, keeping me safe in his love, and guiding me to the next horizon."

For information on how you can help be a part of this great effort to wrap and mail Bibles For The World, or for literature explaining the various ministries of the organization, we invite you to call or write:

**Bibles For The World**
**P. O. Box 36888**
**Colorado Springs, CO  80936-9950**

**Telephone Toll Free:**
**(888) 68-BIBLE (682-4253)**

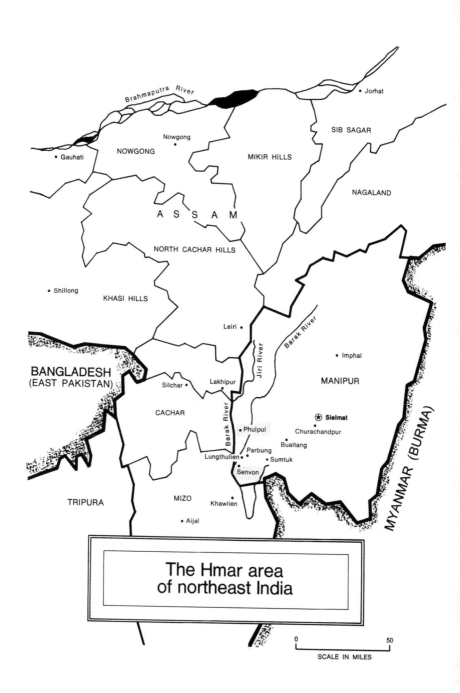

# The Hmar area
## of northeast India

0          50

SCALE IN MILES